P9-BYR-386

"AHEM"

# THE BEAVERTON

PRESENTS

# GLORIOUS AND ~~OR~~ FREE

## THE ~~TRUE~~ HISTORY OF CANADA

**LUKE GORDON FIELD** AND **ALEX HUNTLEY**

*In memory of Laurent Noonan,*
*The Beaverton's founder and publisher who*
*supported this project from its very beginning*

CREDITS

**30,000 Years of History in about Four Pages** / 2 Dino bones: Flickr commons / Tepee: Flickr commons / 3 Longhouse: Gordy, Wilbur F. Stories of American History. New York: Charles Scribner's Sons, 1913. Page 20. / 4 Arrowhead: $1LENCE D00600D, English Wikipedia / 5 Viking Sod House artwork: Jennifer Grant • **First Contact** / 6 Paper: Rijks Museum, object #RP-P-1961-746 / *Histoire de l'Amerique Septentrionale...*: Public Archives of Canada, Ottawa/AP (C-12005) / 8 Ships: ??? / Beaver: Flickr commons / Piano and fish: A Dictionary of Music and Musicians: Volume 1, pg. 702 / Pixabay CCO / Mosquito: ??? / 9 Map artwork: Jennifer Grant / 11 Cartier: Wikipedia commons / 12 Man bearing cross: C.W. Jefferys, LAC C-073576 / 13 Brébeuf and Lalemant: Bibliothéque nationale de France / 14 Officer: LAC C-010368 / 15 Map of part of Acadia: marysrosaries.com • **France Two** / 16 Portrait of Rev. John Stuart: LAC Acc. No. 1989-514-60) / 18 D'Iberville: Wikimedia commons / Magdelaine de Verchères: A Daughter of New France, Arthur G. Doughty / 20 Portrait of a young man in a hat: Jean-Baptiste Greuze, Wikipedia commons / 21 Artwork: Jennifer Grant / 24 Artwork: Jennifer Grant / 25 Exile of the Acadians, Alfred Sandham: LAC C-024549 / 26 Pocket Guide: Library of Congress / Montcalm: Albert Ferland, Wikimedia commons / 27 Ball in cup: Flickr commons / The Death of General Wolfe: Benjamin West, Wikipedia commons / Risk game: Tambako The Jaguar, Flickr commons • **How to Make the French Drink Tea** / 28 Siege of Quebec: LAC C-77769 / 28 Beaver: Flickr commons / Boat: University of Illinois Urbana-Champaign, Flickr Commons / 30 Rebels: Image from page 18 of "The American anti-slavery almanac, for ... : calculated for Boston, New York, and Pittsburgh .." (1836) / Demasduit: Wikimedia commons / 31 Sir Guy Carleton, Wikimedia commons / 33 Declaration of Independence: U.S. National Archives / 36 Family tree, Flickr commons / Edward Percy Moran, Library of Congress, Wikipedia commons / 37 Battle of Queenston: Public Archives of Canada, Ottawa, AP C-276 / 38 Portrait of Sir Isaac Brock: Toronto Public Library / 39 Map of Western British North America, David Thompson, Wikimedia commons / 40 Portrait of John Budden: Glenbow Museum, Calgary (55.31.3) / 42 Artwork: Jennifer Grant / 43 The Tyrone Inn, William James Thomson, Toronto Public Library • **Rebellion, Struggle, and Mutton Chops** / 44 Portrait of William Lyon Mackenzie: Government of Ontario Arts Collection, Queen's Park, Toronto (MGS606898) / Montgomery's Tavern: Charles William Jefferys, Toronto Public Library / Beaver: Flickr commons / 46 Lambton: Wikipedia commons / Lafontaine: Wikipedia commons / Flag: Image from page 183 of Sponsor Souvenir Album: History & Reunion (1895), Flickr commons / 47 The Battle of Saint-Eustachem Wikipedia commons / 48 Ribbons: Shared Shelf

*Credits continue on page 197*

**Principal Authors**
Luke Gordon Field (Editor-in-Chief)
Alex Huntley (Editor)

**Contributors**
Tristan Bradley
Mark Dolynskyj
Adriane Epprecht
Nancy Oakley

**Artwork**
Jennifer Grant

**Editor (Penguin Group)**
Justin Stoller

**Design & Photo Illustrations (Penguin Group)**
Five Seventeen

PENGUIN

an imprint of Penguin Canada, a division of
Penguin Random House Canada Limited

Canada • USA • UK • Ireland • Australia • New Zealand •
India • South Africa • China

First published 2017

Copyright © 2017 by Luke Gordon Field and Alex Huntley

www.penguinrandomhouse.ca

LIBRARY AND ARCHIVES CANADA CATALOGUING IN PUBLICATION

Field, Luke Gordon, author
Glorious and/or free : the true history of Canada /
Luke Gordon Field and Alex Huntley.

Issued in print and electronic formats.
ISBN 978-0-7352-3329-4 (softcover).--ISBN 978-0-7352-3330-0 (EPUB)

1. Canada—History—Humor. 2. Canadian wit and humor (English). I. Huntley, Alex, author II. Title. III. Title: Beaverton presents glorious and/or free.

FC173.F54 2017        971.002'07        C2017-900168-X
                                        C2017-900402-6

Printed and bound in the United States of America

10  9  8  7  6  5  4  3  2  1

 Penguin
Random House
Canada

# CONTENTS

# INTRODUCTION:
## A Guide to Understanding a Non—Heritage Minute History of Canada

Beloved Reader,

Congratulations on your purchase of *Glorious and/or Free*. Unlike what you've experienced in most Canadian history classes, you'll now be required to read a book rather than have a melodramatic Heritage Minute teach you about a brain surgeon who leapt tall buildings while saving PEI from an explosion, or something like that.

Here you'll be reading about Canada's inspiring history as it's found in the archives of our publication, *The Beaverton*. We've also managed to obtain such timeless historical artifacts as letters, posters, photos, paintings, and a half-eaten femur bone from the last Franklin expedition. We'll be reviewing some important dates and turning points in our national story. But why read Canadian history at all?

Because it's amazing! And also your grandmother already bought you this book and she loves you and is going to ask you about it next time you see her, just like she asked you about that sweater she got you last year. Why don't you ever wear that sweater, Kyle?

When we made this book our goal was to transport readers back to grade school to remember what they were taught in Canadian history class. And so what if your teacher was hungover most of the time?

So sit back and relax with a cup of Tim's coffee, put *Hockey Night in Canada* on mute, try to avoid dunking the book in your chalet sauce, and continue to enjoy living on a land that was brutally stolen from Indigenous people through deceit, assault, and outright murder. Because it's about to get real Canadian in here.[1]

Any and all complaints about this book may be sent by mail to:

COMPLAINTS
24 Sussex Drive
Ottawa, ON K1N 6Z7

Sincerely,

The Editors

---

1 Please note this book may contain: Exposure to Canadian history, scenes of gratuitous patriotism, flash photography, traces of gluten, and strong Victorian-era language.

# ~30,000 Years of HISTORY in about 4 Pages.

## (3,200,000,000 BCE–1496)

"What the hell is that?" —God after forgetting he made beavers

Our national tale begins when the first people called "shotgun" on the land that is now Canada. Although there weren't any newspapers or even a CBC, there were Indigenous oral tales of the world's creation, complex societies with their own languages, and interestingly shaped rocks. And because white archeologists have done exhaustive research, they can tell Indigenous people how they once behaved and what many of their traditions were, just in case they forgot. The "staring at stones" scientific method is far superior to any reliance on long-held oral traditions. Why? Because science!

# KEY DATES

**3,200,000,000 BCE**
The last time Earth could
fit into that nice dress since
developing plate tectonics

**500,000 – 50,000 BCE**
The Hot 'n' Spicy BBQ Era

**50,000 – 10,000 BCE**
The Really Cold Era

**13,500 BCE**
Oldest known footprint, smear
marks of a human stepping in
dog shit in British Columbia

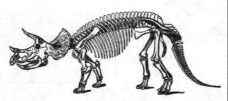

**2114 BCE**
God plants dinosaur fossils near
Drumheller, Alberta to trick non-believers

**1200 CE**
Collapse of the Cree teepee
housing market

# FIRST PEOPLES CROSSED THE BERINGIA WOOED BY ICE

*If there's one thing for certain in the history of Indigenous Canadians, it's that during the last Ice Age their ancestors crossed the glacial land bridge known as the Beringia, lured by North America's bounty of beautiful, breathtaking ice.*

*So why did these people travel thousands of kilometres across a frigid and barren landscape? There are many theories. Some say these people wanted to start bottling glacial ice for its special,* refreshing taste. Others have suggested that they were chasing a special herd of caribou that sustained itself on the ice. And then there are some who say it was a giant bet.

*More radical theories hold that these First Peoples travelled by boat, or that they'd always lived in North America, but the land bridge theory has been repeated by archaeologists for decades so we can just stop thinking about it.*

## Boy disappointed spirit animal is now extinct

———— 4500 BCE ————

SQUAMISH TERRITORY — A teenager whose elders recently assigned him a woolly mammoth as his spirit animal was disappointed to hear that the animal no longer roams the earth.

"I have no idea what it looks like," complained the 15-year-old of his symbolic spiritual representation. "Is it a fish, or some type of bird? No one has seen anything like it in years."

The young man pleaded with his elders to be reassigned a wolf or bear.

"It's not fair—all my friends got to be a whale or an eagle or something cool. Well, at least I'm not a stinkbug like Kevin."

## Inuit surprise party ruined after guests spotted three kilometres away

———— 4000 BCE ————

IGLOOIK ISLAND — The long-planned surprise party celebrating local boy Kayuqtuq's first solo hunting trip was ruined this morning when the 16-year-old saw his would-be party hosts across the vast sheet of ice and rock on which they reside.

"We tried to distract Kayuqtuq from seeing the approaching surprise party grow bigger on the horizon," said father Atiqtallq. "But there are only so many times you can say 'Look behind you!' before a guy catches on."

**"Unfortunately, we had literally nothing to hide behind as we approached."**

Preparations for the bash had gone splendidly. Invitations were sent out to camps across the island, and some of the best throat singers made the journey.

"He wasn't the fastest to grow up," said mother Nanouk. "So when he could finally hold the harpoon by himself without falling over, we wanted to celebrate. Unfortunately, we had literally nothing to hide behind as we approached."

When they realized they'd been spotted, the party yelled "Surprise!" but, at three kilometres away, the shout was lost on the wind.

## An Arrowhead void of any context

## Pictograph vandals strike cave again!

———— 3000 BCE ————

OJIBWA TERRITORY — Another cave has been heavily vandalized by unknown assailants using red ochre. The hoodlums ruined a perfectly good rock wall by drawing a horned snake, five lynx, a man with a spear, and what some speculate is the gang's symbol: a canoe.

# Iroquois lacrosse game lasts two weeks with no clear winner

———— C. 1400 ————

SENECA TERRITORY — A match between the Cayuga Pale Faces and the Seneca Honkies ended in a draw after a 336-hour game.

More than 300 players pursued a clay ball down the two-kilometre field, a chase whose purpose was unknown to all involved. At times, players switched teams in the scrums.

"Overtime is what the game is all about," said Pale Faces captain Kaiiontwa'kon, who made some excellent plays in front of what many believe was the opposing team's net.

**"Overtime is what the game is all about," said Pale Faces captain Kaiiontwa'kon**

Next week, the Honkies will be up against the Oneida Caucasians while the Pale Faces take on the Mohawk Mohawks.

# Viking Sod-House instructions—1000 CE

© VIKEA Systems 1000 CE

## Adopted girl fitting in well with people who murdered her parents

——— SEASON OF THE CORN ———

ONTARIO — A local Huron girl is being praised for her efforts to assimilate with an Iroquois band.

The 12-year-old joined the Mohawk community following a raid on her village that saw her parents brutally murdered right before her eyes. The girl was given a new name and adopted by the warrior who'd killed her father. According to custom, the girl will care for her new parent's household until she's old enough to be married.

"It hasn't been easy, I can tell you that," her adopted father Deganwida said as she made his dinner. "Last week I caught her trying to poison my food and had to severely beat her. But we talked about it afterward and I think we're all good now."

Since the attack a little over two months ago, the girl has attempted to run away four times, destroyed several packs of furs, and set fire to Deganwida's home.

When asked for comment, the girl, who is now known as Genessee, stared blankly into empty space.

## Mass of Cod Sinks Ship

The recent shipwrecking of the San Juan is determined to have been caused by a giant outcrop of solid cod colliding with the ship's hull.

"We were just travelling along, making our usual trip to this new land we found," said crew member Mintxo Etxeberria. "Then all of a sudden we slam into what felt like a brick wall. Turns out that wall was thousands and thousands of cod fish."

Mi'hmaq witnesses in the area described a sudden eddy of cod—a natural but extraordinarily dangerous event for Basque fishermen off the Grand Banks. The solid mass of fish penetrated the ship just below the waterline, causing it to capsize and sink slowly in dark depths of cod.

Luckily, because of the sheer amount of fish, no lives were lost. The Basque fishermen simply walked across the slippery path to reach dry land.

—Grand Banks, Atlantic Ocean

# FIRST CONTACT

## Intercultural Foreplay.

### (1497–1670)

"Tell the natives that they have been living on French territory for the past 10,000 years and that I discovered it for them." —Samuel de Champlain, 1608

We're assuming that, as all Canadians do with history books, you've skipped ahead of the chapter on Indigenous peoples and are now reading your first page. Welcome! As we all know, Canadian history didn't actually start until white Europeans arrived in the 16th century. French, English, Spanish, and even Portuguese explorers flocked to the Americas during the Age of Exploration. And although they spoke different languages and had very different hat styles, they had one goal in common: misnaming an entire race of people forever.

# KEY DATES

## 1534
Jacques Cartier sets sail for discovery with his ships *Câlisse*, *Tabarnak*, and *Criss de calice de tabarnak d'osti de sacrament*

## 1588
Last surviving European beaver killed in a duel with fashionista

## 1608
Scurvy all the rave in Quebec colony

## 1610
Champlain introduces the gun to bring peace to Indigenous community

## 1622
Newfoundland named most unoriginal name for a colony

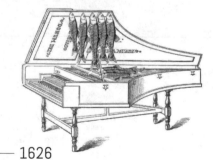

## 1626
Montagnais trade two dozen furs for European-style fish-drying rack

## 1639
New colony of mosquitoes reaches 2,456,323,212 in size

## 1666
Habitants win prolonged battle over patent and copyright to © Pea Soup

# John Cabot's map of Canada

*There are few records of John Cabot's 1497 voyage along Canada's east coast, but this map, drawn by Cabot himself, illustrates that most mapmaking at the time was guesswork.*

# FIRST EUROPEANS CALLED INDIGENOUS PEOPLE "AFRICANS" BEFORE CALLING THEM "INDIANS"

Many have wondered why Indigenous people were called "Indians," but did you know that the first European explorers and colonizers first called them "Africans" in the belief that they'd reached a colder version of that continent? Lacking any better locution, the French, English, and Dutch all used this dated and offensive term.

In 1667, however, a coureur de bois named Samuel Jean Lavoie, who was living with a group of "Africans," concluded that the first explorers had gotten it wrong. "Instead of landing on the continent of Africa," wrote Lavoie in a letter to his sister, "Cartier clearly landed in India. We should be calling these people Indians rather than a name based on a white man's ignorance."

Lavoie was determined to change the moniker, but that would require convincing many in the colonies who thought "Africans" was fine and that Lavoie was just being politically correct. The governor of New France, Daniel de Rémy de Courcelle, also resisted the idea, given that he'd named his billiard team "The Quebec Africans" and that many merchants had been using the term to sell such products as African corn, African tobacco, and large wooden African man statues.

That didn't stop Lavoie, who continued to raise awareness of the issue. Finally, in 1670, King Louis XIV decreed that "Africans" was an offensive term, that the continent on which New France was situated was probably a part of India, and that the Indigenous people would henceforth be known as "Indians."

For their part, native people continued to use the term "white devil" as a moniker for the Europeans.

## IN THE NEWS

Champlain to name island after 12-year-old wife, Hélène

Catholic Church demands Indian women stop having Frenchmen's babies

Crew on Cabot's ship not as excited about Cod as he thought they'd be

Manitoba can't wait to be discovered

## Aboriginals overwhelmed by superiority of Western suffering

——— DECEMBER 29, 1608 ———

QUEBEC CITY — Admitting they couldn't take it anymore, local Algonquins have finally given French colonists their robes and crops just to ease their obvious suffering.

"Sure, we could have just murdered them, or let nature do it for us," said a member of the tribe. "But the sheer force of their misery drove us back.

"We ended up giving them half of our stuff and some tea just to stop the moaning."

The French, at first confused by such poor military tactics, soon concluded that the Indigenous people's primitive society lacked the structure necessary to systematically oppress and marginalize minority groups the way Europe does.

"They must be fools to allow a people who pray to a different God and refuse to assimilate into their society to live among them," said colonist Philippe DeNeige. "But this tea does make my smallpox sores hurt less."

The French were planning on repaying the Algonquin for their assistance by giving them trinkets, beads, and a variety of European diseases.

# The Jesuits are coming!

*In the 17th century, France's Jesuit Catholics had grown tired of murdering Protestants and non-believers in Europe. They wanted to stretch their legs, explore the world, and murder people who did not agree with their beliefs in a more exotic location. One such man was Pierre Biard, who kept a diary of his journey. His entry from September 22, 1611, follows.*

—

It has been four months since I arrived in this new land, and I continue to thank the Lord for his choice to guide me here. Every day in France was the same. Wake up, cut off the toes of a Protestant, have lunch, whip a sodomite, eat dinner, go to sleep. I always felt there had to be something more to being a slavishly devout, unquestioningly dogmatic Catholic.

But no longer! This land is my fresh start. A chance to get to know the world (and in the process maybe find myself), and to impose my own version of the religion that has killed millions back home. I am so excited.

And the people here are wonderful! Not stuck up and reserved like those in France. They live for the now, for the individual moments that make life special. It is so exhilarating to take that feeling away from them by teaching them about the absurd cruelty that is the one true God.

I should go now and rest. Tomorrow I have a big day teaching the natives about Jesus's famous proverb: "Beat thy brother with a stick until thy brother stops moving and then beat thy brother once more for good measure."

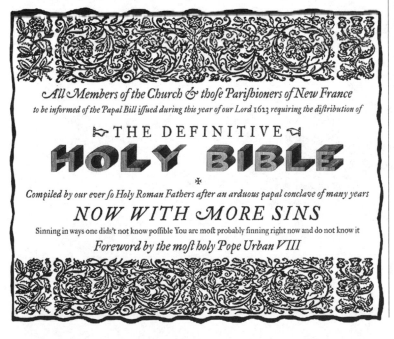

*All Members of the Church & those Parishioners of New France*
to be informed of the Papal Bill issued during this year of our Lord 1613 requiring the distribution of

### ☞ THE DEFINITIVE ☜

# HOLY BIBLE
✳
*Compiled by our ever so Holy Roman Fathers after an arduous papal conclave of many years*

## NOW WITH MORE SINS
Sinning in ways one did's not know possible You are most probably sinning right now and do not know it
*Foreword by the most holy Pope Urban VIII*

PROFILE

## Young Jacques Cartier

The man who would become synonymous with the discovery and exploration of Canada was born in Brittany, France, in 1491. As a child, young Jacques loved three things: playing with his friends, exploring the coastline, and kidnapping things to hold for ransom.

"My little Jacques stole the neighbour boy's dog again," his mother, Hélène, wrote in her diary. "He didn't give it back until the family gave him all the sweets they had in their house."

Cartier, known throughout Brittany as "le petit fucker," would steal animals, beloved dolls, and younger siblings so that he could blackmail their owners/loved ones for ever-increasing amounts. Having continued this practice throughout his childhood and adolescence, he was able to raise enough money to buy his first ship.

Undoubtedly, the success of his exploits in the Old World influenced his strategy in the New, which mainly consisted of grabbing Aboriginal chiefs and bringing them as trophies back to France, where they all inevitably died of disease.

# Notre Dame Society founds Montreal as colony exclusively for devout Christians and drunk university students

MAY 17, 1642

MONT ROYAL — The Société de Notre-Dame has established a colony in Montreal on the condition that its only inhabitants be those Christians blessed with "purity of spirit" and intoxicated students looking for a good time.

"In the name of our Father, the Lord in heaven, we have come here together this day to consecrate sacred ground. Ground that shall be walked on only by those handpicked by Jesus Christ," said founder Jerome Le Royer. "And by Boston College students named Chad who wish to enjoy our lower drinking age.

"In heaven's name we pray that Chad and his bros don't get lost on their way to the rippers," he added.

In accordance with the colony's charter, residents will be governed by a strict moral and legal code that requires Montrealers to pray multiple times a day, confess their sins regularly, and not cheap out when it's their turn to buy a round at Peel Pub. Newly arrived residents like Jean Abadie were clearly excited by the prospect of living in such a holy city.

"I have asked the Lord many times to be taken away from the wickedness of France. Now he has seen fit to create this garden for me and my family. Also, I could totally use some pizza to soak up this J.D. if you wanna come."

At press time, Montreal officials said they would be open to expanding their citizenry to include people who make poorly built roads and bridges.

# Dragging a heavy wooden cross everywhere now a requirement for all new settlers, says de Maisonneuve

# Almighty God rewards Jesuits with torture

———— MARCH 17, 1649 ————

HURONIA — The Almighty Lord today rewarded two of his humble servants spreading the Word of God with the most terrible, agonizing torture and death.

The Heavenly Father honoured Brother Jean de Brébeuf and Brother Gabriel Lalemant for their decades of religious study, fasting, teaching, grovelling, and genuflecting when he instructed the Iroquois to kidnap the pair during a raid on St. Louis. Brébeuf and Lalemant thanked the Lord for being blessed with a horrific demise.

As their captors led them to their village, the martyrs-to-be shed tears of joy that they'd been chosen by Him and wondered aloud whether they'd be boiled in oil as John the Apostle was by the Romans or be thrown into a furnace like Shadrach, Meshach, and Abednego when they refused to bow down to King Nebuchadnezzar. Or, perhaps they'd be bludgeoned by an axe and beaten to death like St. Alphege after he declined to pay ransom to Viking raiders.

Brother Lalemant was reportedly heard saying, "Please, oh Lord, do not go easy on us! We are not fitting of a quick beheading or arrow to the heart. Please let us suffer for days on end and undergo the most awful fate."

God heard the pleas of the Jesuits and did instruct the Iroquois to beat them with large sticks before ritualistically removing their skin with broken shells, a fate similar to St. Bartholomew's, which made the French missionaries feel honoured by the Almighty. Then God commanded the Iroquois to pour boiling water over their bodies, bringing a smile to the martyrs' bloody faces.

According to witnesses, Brébuf and Lalemant said they were looking forward to having a remaining charred piece of their bones idolized for years to come.

Upon hearing of the two martyrs' fate, fellow Jesuit Thomas Bouchard, based in Acadia, was seen asking a friendly group of Mi'kmaq whether he could share the same fate.

# Fresh floozies arrive from France!

AUGUST 2, 1663

QUEBEC — Men of all rank and station lined the banks of the St. Lawrence, bursting with excitement as the first boatload of filles du roi docked and began to unload. These fresh walking baby-makers are up for grabs to the highest bidder, and all manner of men, from habitants to seigneurs, have been assembling since dawn to get the first look at the goods.

"You have no idea how happy I am," said one Jean-Paul Mourin, a merchant who arrived in New France some 12 years ago. "I've had to use trees . . . creatively; I don't even remember what a woman looks like!"

"The king says these women come from only the purest, most chaste brothels, asylums, and orphanages in Paris," declared Intendant Jean Talon to the eager men as the women queued up to be married. "We brought you the ones with the least amount of abscesses and carbuncles. And there's no way they're going to leave you, since we bought them only a one-way ticket."

Talon, who instigated the royal decree to import the woman flesh, has been nominated for the highest award in the new colony. An estimated 800 more loose ladies are expected to arrive over the next decade.

# Fashionable French troops freeze to death in très chic fall uniforms

## Iroquois intimidated by perishing soldiers' avant-garde style

JANUARY 5, 1666

FORT ST. LOUIS — Strutting their effortless, haute couture designs, the trendy Carignan-Salières Regiment froze to death in fashion as they wandered the woods looking to defeat the Iroquois.

Bucking the predictable snowshoes-and-heavy-coats approach, the first uniformed regiment in Canada opted to sport moccasins and maintain their traditional fall uniform—a bold statement, particularly in −30°C weather.

"The brown-and-grey patterns of the vests are totally to die for and to die in," explained Sergeant Jean "LaFleur" Darbois, the Saurel Company's fashion designer. "Contrasting two colours and having no interior lining is all the rage these days."

> "The brown-and-grey patterns of the vests are totally to die for and to die in," explained Sergeant Jean "LaFleur" Darbois, the Saurel Company's fashion designer.

The 24 cleverly placed buttons along their outer vests may not have protected them against the cold, but they certainly protected the shivering soldiers from being passé.

Complementing their vests and single wool blanket were sleek white cravats—coarse cloth for the men, crêpe de chine for the officers—which cleverly matched the bright white snow that slowly consumed them. In addition, the retro slouch hats gave the troops a rugged look with their frostbitten noses and bloody, chapped lips.

The man responsible for the ill-fated campaign, New France's Governor Daniel de Rémy de Courcelle, says that although everyone died of the cold, at least their fashion was hot.

# Events in Acadia

*As the Jan Brady of French colonies in North America, Acadia is often overlooked by historians, who tend to focus on the shapely hips and beautiful blue eyes of Quebec. But Acadia actually had quite a lot going on, as this map illustrates.*

New dyke system ensures farm's prosperity until the next time it's burned

1659 – 428th resident conceived here

1645 – Charles d'Aulnay loses civil war, forced to become governor

1628 – Wandering British accidentally conquer colony

1642 – Few hours of peace between warring families possibly occurred

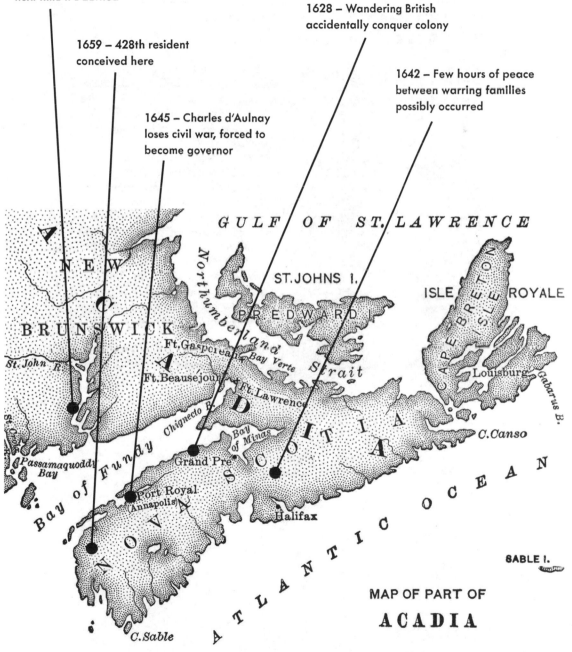

MAP OF PART OF
**ACADIA**

Numb. 517

# The Beaver Town Gazette.

### Published by a Trusted Source of News

From Tuesday July 29, O. S. to Saturday Auguſt. 9, N. S. July 29, O. S. 1670

## French prieſt who doeſn't know Latin juſt wings it.

*Trois Rivières, Aug. 3*

**M**arek Antoine-Lavalin, aged 25, from the region of Lyon, conducted his firſt maſs at Trois Rivières this week in a complete, unadulterated, made-up language that ſort of ſounded like it could be Latin.

"I tried my beſt to learn Latin during ſeminary but it juſt never ſtuck," ſaid Antoine-Lavalin. "Fortunately, when I got to the colony I diſcovered I could juſt ſcat with words that ended in a vowel and no one knew the difference."

As he roſe to the pulpit of his new church in Trois-Rivières, Antoine-Lavalin glanced around the congregation and attempted to ſuſs out those who might be able to tell the difference between mumbo-jumbo rambling and honeſt-to-God Latin. There was one older, ſlightly well-dreſsed gentleman who made the prieſt a bit nervous, as his tights were unbeſplattered with mud and his face had a certain educated air. Nonetheleſs, Antoine-Lavalin ſteeled himself and began the ſervice:

*In nominay Patrice, ate fillie, ate Spiritus Sanctimonius*
*Spaghetti agnacianominus piccolo noſtradamus, utalan ſimon and ſacrificial myſtery celebrandium*
*Confetti deo impotente ate vorbis, duce, quoa pecker vie numb-nuts.*
*My cuppa, my cuppa, my maximus cuppa*

**A**fter intoning this opening call, Antoine-Lavalin peeked at the congregation. He was ſatiffied that nobody knew or cared about the difference, and that half of them were already aſleep.

[Price 2 ſpruce.]

# FRANCE

## (1670–1763)

## 2 TWO

"Look, I love France. You know that. Everybody knows that. But I have to say, there's something about this Canada country that really does something for me. It's kind of exotic and foreign. And I can tell it's into me, too." —King Louis XIV of France, 1660

Beginning in the mid-17th century, King Louis XIV of France decided to take a firmer hand in the management of his country and empire. His first task was to come up with a name for its fledgling colonial enterprise. His counsellors recommended calling it the "Fuck You English" territories. The Church preferred the more elegant "Catholic Land." Louis, however, insisted on naming it "France Two."

"France Two is the perfect name for our colony in the Americas," Louis was heard remarking one evening. "It tells people that this colony is France, but like a second one. Like if France was happening all over again. It's great."

Signs were soon erected, and the name found much favour among the colonists. Even today, centuries after the English conquered the land and renamed it Lower Canada, French Canadians commonly refer to themselves as citizens of France Two. "Bring Back France Two!" was a familiar rallying cry during the sovereignty referendums of 1980 and 1995. But the question remains: What was life actually like for the people living in that colony? We're here to fill in the details.

# KEY DATES

**1688**
D'Iberville launches second expedition
to Hudson Bay to find lost wallet

**1692**
French announce new fort defence
strategy: heroic 14-year-old girls

**1744–48**
European nations lose track of which
other nations they're fighting

**1747**
Louisbourg surrenders to
passing herd of deer

**1752**
*Halifax Gazette* publishes region's
first sponsored content

# FRANCE TWO'S CURRENCY

Quebec was a more egalitarian society than France, with only eight different classes of noblemen instead of the traditional fourteen. (There were also the fur-trading merchants and the "technically-not-slaves" peasants.) The colonial elite of Quebec didn't add money to the economy per se, but they created a ton of "brand value" and "name recognition."

Although much of the economy ran on a barter system, the colony did have its own currency, called the buffon, which was made by cutting different types of wood into circles. Confusingly, all the circles were the same size; the only way to tell the value of a given coin was to know what type of wood it was. One maple was equal to 10 spruce, which was worth between 39 and 42 cedar depending on the day's exchange rate. Lack of basic wood knowledge led to frequent confusion.

# Madam LaFontaine thinks she's so great just because all her kids are still alive

*by Marie Benoit*

— MAY 4, 1667 —

I'm so sick and tired of Francine LaFontaine and her holier-than-thou attitude. She walks around with her nose in the air, acting like she's better than the other women in the colony just because all her children remain living.

> "I get it, lady — your kids are alive. La-di-da."

Don't get me wrong, I'm happy she hasn't had a child die during its infancy. And I do recognize that she is literally the only woman in the colony who can say that. But that doesn't mean she's superior to the rest of us; she just got lucky.

The other day I ran into her at the market and she just would not stop. "Maxime, my eldest who is still alive . . . Teddy the little scamp who is still alive . . . Tiffany the heartbreaker who is still alive." I get it, lady—your kids are alive. La-di-da.

Your children's ability to survive the epidemics, farming accidents, and birthing process that have claimed 80% of the other kids is great, it really is. But you don't need to talk about it constantly. Just like I don't constantly brag to everyone how I still have most of my teeth. Some things you keep to yourself.

Plus, I bet Francine wouldn't be acting so high and mighty if she'd seen how her husband had been staring at my chompers.

# Trust Exercises

*In addition to its peasants and merchants, France Two was home to as many as 1200 indentured servants who worked on seigneuries in order to pay off debts or contracts. A crucial element of this system was trust between the servant and the seigneur. Fortunately, the colony developed a number of activities the two parties could do together to build up their relationship.*

## Oldest man in Quebec, aged 27, passes away

—— DECEMBER 16, 1697 ——

VILLE DE QUEBEC — After living for almost three decades, during which he saw things current residents of the colony know only from history books, Gilles Bouchelu died after a long battle with illness at the ripe old age of 27—the oldest recorded age in this new colony.

"Can you believe that when he was born the Edict of Nantes still existed? And Clement IX was pope, not Clement X!" said daughter Clarisse.

With years of experience as a manual labourer, Bouchelu came to the colony at the age of 13 from the Lyon region of France. His tireless efforts helped shape the area's settlement. With luck and by the grace of God, he survived scurvy, Iroquois attacks, dysentery, and even witchcraft, finally passing away of old age.

He leaves a legacy of sage advice and sets an age benchmark to which we can all aspire. Bouchelu is survived by his two daughters, nine grandchildren, and eight great-grandchildren.

---

## Truſt Exercises for Indentured Servants

Upon the obtainment of new indentured ſervants, who ſhall be of vital aſſiſtance to the *habitants* in developing the wealth potential of the ſeigneurie, the following truſt exerciſes are recommended to better acclimatize the ſervant to the culture of the ſeigneurie.

### THE BLIND FALL

*Time required: two ſhakes of a lamb's tail*

Have the indentured ſervant fall backward with his eyes cloſed. Make ſure to not catch him or prevent injury in any way.

### RUNNING FREE

*Time required: ten ſeconds*

Tell the ſervants that they're free to leave as long as they can run off the ſeigneurie property before you count to 10.

*Note: It's very important that this task be impoſſible to achieve. Start the exercise at the bottom of the property and have them run along the length of the land away from the water.*

Fun Tip! Add a blindfold to make this exerciſe extra entertaining.

### EYE CONTACT

*Time required: until you get the meſſage across*

Making eye contaƈt is ſometimes difficult for people, as it involves a certain amount of truſt and reſpeƈt. This aƈtivity will enſure that no one develops the nerve or confidence to exchange looks with you or anyone else, thus preventing the poſſibility of collaboration and/or insolence.

Pair the indentured ſervants and have them face each other. If there's an odd number, conſider pairing a ſervant with your horſe, as you muſt teach him to reſpeƈt the beaſt. If they raiſe their eyes to glance into their partner's eyes, bring down the whip and ſpare no fury. Avoiding eye contact, relying on ſidelong glances, and exhibiting ſatisfaƈtory ſubſervience will become ſecond nature in no time.

### THE STRAW BUILDING

*Time required: three minutes*

Teamwork ſhould be discouraged, as it may develop into friendſhips that could undermine the ſeigneurial ſyſtem.

Pair off the ſervants and tell them they've got five minutes to conſtruƈt a miniature houſe using only the pile of ſtraw before them. After three minutes, inform them that their time has lapsſed and that ſometimes life is not fair. Have each ſervant deſcribe the failings of his partner. Set all the projeƈts on fire.     ——1680.

*from the deſk of Louis de Buade de Frontenac —— Governor General of New France*

# 1715 Fashion: Fresh beaver hats all the rage

*Castor Sauvage Hats newest European fashion trend*

## Fortress Rules

*France Two's primary means of defence was the series of military forts it constructed throughout its territory. Although centrally run, each individual fort was responsible for its own discipline and maintenance.*
*To ensure order, the forts created rules for inhabitants to live by, such as those listed below.*

———

On this glorious day of April the 3rd of the 11th year of the 1700th century at Fortress Louisbourg, we forthwith declare the following rules to govern our mighty refortified fort in the eyes of God and under the grace of our mighty Louis the XIV, may he never die.

Absolutely no playing the fife before 9:30 a.m. and after 9:31 a.m. This is your FINAL WARNING, Jean-Louis.

Whenever the men are absent, the women and children should inquire, "Where are the men?"

Always give the British the fort it and when they make an appearance.

The password of the day shall always be "Password" or "Open the door or I'll shoot."

Kids should be up and whiskyed by 11:00 a.m.

There will be no riding the rapids on bits of wood.

The official order of uniform: stockings first, then breeches.

# Undercover nuns bust sinners' ring

———— SEPTEMBER 4, 1717 ————

MONTREAL — Plain-clothed nuns have announced that they broke a sophisticated sinners' ring yesterday after months of surveillance and evidence gathering.

At church headquarters Ursuline nuns showcased the collected evidence to the public, which included a drawing of breasts not associated with an art piece, two Protestant Bibles, and non-sacramental wine.

"Our team, composed of 12 highly trained nuns, has watched these heretics for months," explained Mother Superior Marie Emmanuelle Marcellette, head of the Morality Enforcement Squad. "We had someone on the inside while our surveillance team watched the activities from church steeples. Once it became apparent that the group was planning to spread demonry, lax morals, and a casual approach to a life of suffering, we knew we had to move in."

The trap was set when an undercover nun posing as a coureur du bois arranged a meeting with the five men to smoke tobacco. The Ursulines, who were waiting with beating sticks and rosaries, promptly apprehended the accused.

Charges against the five include 87 counts of blasphemy, 3 counts of being a Huguenot, 10 counts of failing to comply with orders of Bishop Jean-Baptiste de la Croix de Chevrière de St. Vallier, and 1 count of littering.

The presumed guilty will make an appearance at Sovereign Council tomorrow where they will be found more formally guilty and receive severe punishment.

# Converting the Indigenous

———— JANUARY 4, 1721 ————

*The following is an excerpt from the diary of junior missionary Edmond Lecalvier, who describes his superior's attempts to convert a local Aboriginal.*

—

Father Patrice greeted the man and introduced me to him as Bear Eye. His skin was red like the devil and his neck was dangerously unbowed. The two of them sat together as the Father explained the religion Bear Eye was to join.

"You shall worship but one God, the true God, who sent his only son Jesus to die for your sins."

"So I worship only this one God," replied Bear Eye. "I do not worship his son, who is not a God?"

"No, you worship his son, too."

"I'm confused."

"It doesn't matter," said Father Patrice. "The point is to follow the lessons his son has taught us, like in that book I showed you."

"Yes. I liked the words the son spoke. But I was confused. Your religion teaches you to love your enemies?"

"Yes. That is the only way one can know true salvation."

"Last week I saw your soldiers cut a man's testicles out for speaking English," said Bear Eye.

"Shit gets real in these streets," said Father Patrice [*Editor's note: Are you sure about this translation?*]. "All we can do is try our best. The most important thing is spreading Jesus's message to people who haven't yet heard it."

"Is that why you keep kidnapping children from my village?"

"Look, do you want to get into heaven or not?"

Bear Eye refused the Father and excused himself. Father Patrice and I could only shake our heads and wonder what it would take to convince these savages.

# Angry mother calls son by using all of his 329 middle and family names

———— OCTOBER 22, 1723 ————

SAGUENAY — After finding her son asleep and intoxicated in the barn, local matriarch Renée Isabeau began to bellow all of his 329 proper names—a feat that, since last checked, was still in progress.

"Louis-Olivier Félix Jean-Baptiste Pierre Philippe," she began. "François Claude Baudouin Christophe Clément Alain Armand Gilbert Arnaud Bertrand Émile Étienne Rodrigue Théodore Stéphane Frédéric Hubert Gerard Aristide Théophane Valentin Victor Jules Baptiste Octave Antoine Charles Henri Paul Maurice Ignace Guillaume McJagger Benoit Toussaint Lubin-Aubin Alphonse Césaire Hippolyte Ferdinand Ambroise Keith Richards Eudes Bastien Gustave Artus Jean-Jacques Nicolas Guillaume-Charles Maximilien-Lazare Firmin Noel Denys . . . "

Eventually, Isabeau added, "Just wait until your father, Félix Jean-Baptiste Pierre Philippe . . . hears about this."

# La Vérendrye threatens to turn back canoe if sons don't stop asking "Are we there yet?"

———— JUNE 18, 1732 ————

LAKE OF THE WOODS — Pierre Gaultier de Varennes, sieur de La Vérendrye, has had just about enough from sons Jean-Baptiste, François, and Louis-Joseph.

> "I'm going to turn this canoe around," said La Vérendrye

"Ça *suffit!*" said an angry La Vérendrye, giving his paddle an exasperated slap. "Do you see an endless sea stretching all the way to India? We aren't 'there yet'; besides, we don't even know where 'there' is.

"If you don't stop complaining, I'm going to turn this canoe around," he added.

After a month travelling aimlessly upriver, La Vérendrye has grown increasingly irritated with his whiny sons. Jean-Baptiste won't stop arguing that each new lake is the Pacific Ocean; Louis-Joseph drags his end of the canoe on portage; and François keeps kicking the back of his father's seat.

"If you three don't fix your attitudes, I'm going to leave you with the Sioux," said a frustrated La Vérendrye.

Sources say the explorer expects to reach the Pacific in the next few days.

# African woman burns down Montreal for no reason whatsoever

———— APRIL 10, 1734 ————

MONTREAL — In a brutal arson attack, local woman Marie-Joseph Angelique set fire to a house she was staying in of her own free will and then let the flames spread to other homes, causing a blaze that has nearly ruined Montreal.

"This was a depraved and treacherous act," said fire constable Henri DuMonde. "Marie-Joseph had been allowed to live in this house entirely rent-free in exchange for a measly 18 hours a day of chores. But then when the owners told her she'd be transferred to a different house to live rent-free, she got mad and did this.

"It just goes to show how sometimes you can be too nice," he noted.

Once set, the fire spread quickly across rue Saint-Joseph, destroying homes, hospitals, and numerous whips and chains. Residents were outraged by this cowardly crime.

"I can't believe it. It was almost like she was so furious at an oppressive, ruthless society that she wanted to watch it all come down," said neighbour Sarah Lacroix.

# Pornographic Playing Cards

*Despite the colony's conservative, puritanical views, artifacts prove that interest in sex and sexual images remained high. Below are a series of risqué playing cards found on a fur trader near Huronia in 1759.*

# Letter to Governor Cornwallis of Nova Scotia from Colony HR

OCTOBER 3, 1749

*The first governor of Halifax, General Cornwallis, attempted to use scalping as a tactic to terrorize and intimidate the Acadians and their Mi'kmaq allies during frontier warfare. However, he failed to run it by the Colonial Human Resources Department. They were none too pleased.*

—

Lt. General Edward Cornwallis

Re: "Scalping Mi'kmaq for Money"

Sir,

As the new human resources adviser for the colony of Nova Scotia, I implore you to reconsider your proclamation of 12 pence for every Mi'kmaq scalp collected. While we recognize the importance of defending new settlers from ongoing attacks, this order may conflict with the colony's shared corporate values that were set out in the "Growing Together: Corporate Social Responsibility" pamphlet we provided you earlier this year.

As a refresher, it is inconsiderate to remove someone's scalp for the purposes of starting a race war on the Nova Scotian peninsula, as it may encourage revenge attacks against our own settlers. Furthermore, we have no way of determining whether the scalps actually belong to the Mi'kmaq, nor do we have any place to store said scalps within our fair settlements. The colony of Nova Scotia prides itself on being a scalping-free destination and we would like to keep it as such.

May I also note that we now offer employees free training seminars, entitled "How to Make Your Colony Scalping Free," as well as sensitivity training on Acadian and Mi'kmaq culture.

For future proclamations on scalping, colonization, and smallpox, please consult one of our HR advisers. We would be more than happy to assist you.

Your
Servant,

Edwin Rupert Cobb
Human Resources Adviser
Colony of Halifax

# THE SEVEN YEARS' WAR

*The battle for Canada was an epic showdown that the world had not seen for over thirty months, and wouldn't see again for two to three years. England vs. France. Speed vs. strength. Red coat vs. giant white wig.*

*Monocle on the left eye vs. monocle on the right eye. Oppressing Indigenous people vs. oppressing Indigenous people harder. Who would win this clash of titans? England. England won.*

## British cast Acadians into some of the world's highest tides

——— AUGUST 4, 1755 ———

CHIGNECTO, BAY OF FUNDY — The famous whimsy of the British was in full force this year when they selected the Bay of Fundy as the site from which to cast out the pesky Acadians.

Having the world's highest tides, the Bay of Fundy offers an outstanding natural phenomenon in its role as host to an outstanding unnatural deportation. Low tide provided the perfect opportunity to saunter along the ocean's bed, collect shells, and kick out 11,500 people from where they were born.

"It was breathtaking," said Colonel Robert Monckton of the first wave of expulsion, which occurred at 6:48 a.m. on the banks of Chignecto. "And the bay made everything easier. We just walked the Acadians out at low tide and waited for the sea to take them away."

The sheer awesome power of a 50-foot-high wall of water that rises and falls in under 13 minutes was sure to capture the wonder and imagination of those Acadians tossed into its waves.

"After this we'll be deporting Acadians from Grand-Pré, and then from Piziquid. We'll round things off with a grand finale in Annapolis Royal," said Monckton. "But starting the expulsion here, at the site of the world's most impressive tides, was special—even magical—for everyone involved."

# General Louis-Joseph de Montcalm's Pocket Guide to Defending a Fixed Position

*Before he heroically led the French to abysmal defeat in the Battle of the Plains of Abraham, General Montcalm wrote a handy guide for soldiers on how to defend an elevated fortress from enemy approach. Here's the first page of the guide, which hasn't been used in military academies since 1759.*

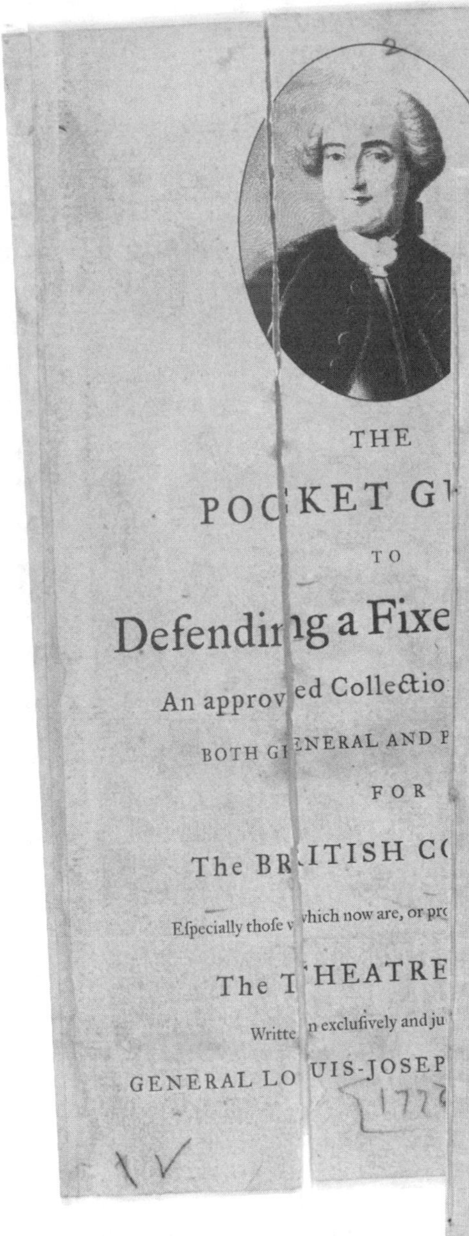

THE

POCKET G

TO

Defending a Fixe

An approved Collectio

BOTH GENERAL AND P

FOR

The BRITISH CO

Especially those which now are, or pro

The THEATRE

Written exclufively and ju

GENERAL LOUIS-JOSEP

1777

## INTRODUCTION.

IF THE ROLE of defending a fixed pofition is in your hands, then fo is this guide. There will be many out there who'll tell you that a fixed pofition, fuch as a walled fortrefs on a cliff, is a fimple thing to defend. They'll fay that you fhould just ftay inside the walls, protected, and rain cannon fire down on anyone who paffes. But they would be cowards.

In this guide you'll learn the true fecret to mounting a defence that's not only victorious but will bring you the perfonal glory you've always dreamed of attaining.

STEP ONE: Fight your enemy on their terms. Your enemy is expecting to mount a long fiege of the fortrefs. In truth, they'd like nothing more than a quick, decifive battle. But as the old adage goes: Be careful what you wifh for. So go give them hell.

STEP TWO: Ufe only inexperienced foldiers. Having an army of well-heeled combat vets is a huge miftake. Sure, they know how to actually shoot their rifles and don't run away as much, but they also tend to claim a lot of credit for victories. That credit fhould be going to you.

STEP THREE: Abandon the high ground as quickly as poffible. Although a lot of people think having the high ground makes it eafier to fire upon your opponent, they're ignoring a crucial element: What if your foldiers flip and tumble down?

STEP FOUR: Make your attack as disorganized and chaotic as poffible. It'll totally throw off your enemy.

## Wolfe somehow dies in battle after holding giant "I am General Wolfe" target on self

# France loses Seven Years' War after poor roll of the die, placing armies in Iceland

——— FEBRUARY 10, 1763 ———

PARIS — The seven-year game that has embroiled Britain, Prussia, Hanover, France, Saxony, Sweden, Austria, Russia, and even Spain took a surprising turn after France suffered an unfortunate roll of the die.

The country had it rough from the get-go, having been unlucky in the opening draw for territory and a seeming magnet for infantry cards. The French and British fought hard over the North American domain, with each turn a nail-biter as armies ceded and regained land. But the deciding loss was owed to a devastating throw of two fours

and a three, forcing France to withdraw all armies to Iceland.

"This game was so rigged against me," complained France's King Louis XV to the other sovereigns. "You all had it out for me, I know it. The Ottomans didn't even attack anyone and it's totally not fair that the British got both Eastern and Western Australia!"

Determined to cut his losses, Louis XV negotiated to take back the sugar colonies of Martinique and Guadalupe by ceding Louisiana to Spain and giving up all hope of regaining North America from Britain.

Feeling relatively sore about the loss and resisting all urges

to flip the board like Hanover did last time, France muttered something about never wanting that "few acres" of snow anyway.

"But we still control the North American jewel, St. Pierre and Miquelon," added the Bourbon king.

VILLE DE QUÉBEC    No. 3

THE

*Beaverton* GAZETTE

MONDAY, *September* 18, 1775.

# Catholic French Canadian torn on which anglophone proteſtant invader to ſupport

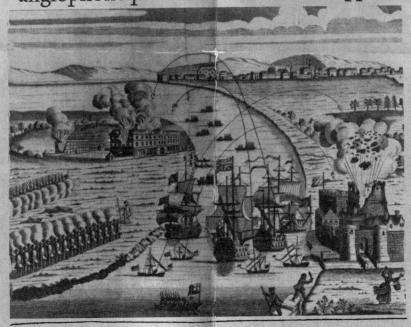

Local man and devout Catholic Jacob Gagnon has admitted that he's having a tough time chooſing whether to ſide with the American Proteſtants who are invading Quebec in the hope of convincing the locals to join their Revolution or the Britiſh Proteſtants who invaded Quebec a few years ago.

"Oh man, tough call," said Gagnon. "On the one hand you have the Britiſh, who don't reſpect my linguiſtic or religious rights. And on the other you have the Americans, who ſeem to view Catholiciſm as a diſeaſe and who ſpeak even leſs French than the Britiſh.

"I juſt don't know where my heart is on this one."

Gagnon was initially leaning toward the Americans due to the fa{ that Britiſh ſoldiers had killed his father at the Plains of Abraham. But hearing of the Americans' deſecration of Roman Catholic ſhrines and general hoſtility toward people who pronounce the word "oui" like they're honking a horn threw him into a grey area.

"Any chance the Spaniſh will make a play for Quebec? I could ſee that working," said Gagnon.

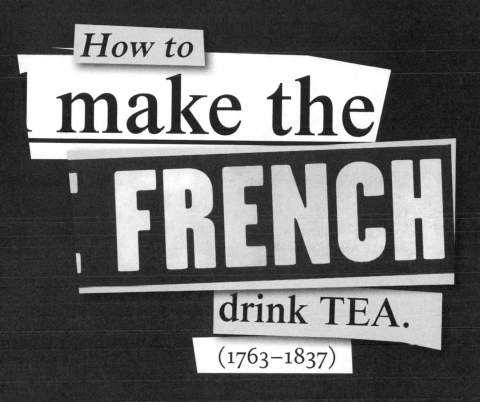

# How to make the FRENCH drink TEA.

## (1763–1837)

"We must anglicize the Québécois by destroying the seigneuries and the Church. If we do not get rid of the French language, generations of British governors will be forced to learn the difference between accent aigu and accent grave." —Governor General Guy Murray

The British soon learned that their victory over the French at the Plains of Abraham had come at a price: spending a lot of time around French people they couldn't kill. To adapt to their new circumstances, the most brutal empire since Rome tried a new tactic: not being total assholes all the time. It did not work out well.

# KEY DATES

**1775**
American rebels invade
Montreal's strip clubs

**1778**
Privateer Stan Rogers of the *Antelope*
wishes he was in Sherbrooke now

**1783**
British North America launches noise
complaint about new disruptive,
unruly neighbour to the south

**1785**
John Molson develops sawdust flavoured
beer for five cents a hogshead

**1791**
Britain creates Upper Canada, Lower
Canada, and Rock Bottom Canada
(previously known as Nova Scotia)

**1815**
War of 1812 ends three years late

**1829**
Labrador Yellow Fox, Newfoundland
Beothuk feared extinct

# THE ODD COUPLE: BRITAIN AND QUEBEC

One was uptight, Protestant, and hated Natives. The other was messy, Catholic, and hated Natives. How would this odd couple handle becoming roommates? They wouldn't have long to make it work. A mere 12 years after Britain's victory in the war gave it control of Canada, it faced a crisis among the American colonies. There, established merchants and politicians began to protest against Britain's taxation and military presence. But although they'd never admit it, what truly angered men like Benjamin Franklin and Thomas Jefferson was the fact that Britain had been cheating on them with Quebec. Their fury boiled over after the Quebec Act of 1774 officially elevated the French Canadian province to "wifey" status. War followed shortly thereafter.

The revolution would have a huge impact on Canada. First, Canadians had to choose whether to join in the fun even though they'd been picked last for the American team. Then, when the colonies ultimately prevailed, a massive influx of Americans loyal to the British Crown flooded across the border. Plus, the price of American cotton went way up.

## All English signage must be three times larger than French, says Governor General

MARCH 3, 1766

QUEBEC CITY — Governor General Guy Carleton has decreed that any and all signage posted in Quebec must be written three times larger in English than the same signage written in French.

This one step, according to Carlton, will help impose Anglo-Saxon culture on Quebec's inhabitants, ensuring that they'll understand and use the new official language in their everyday lives.

"When members of the French race see that their language is inferior in size, they are sure to assimilate," Carlton explained. "'Du thé' will be known as 'tea,' 'le roi' will be 'king,' and 'l'Église catholique' shall be known as 'the Protestant Church,' and so forth."

The new decree will be enforced by the recently created Quebec Office for the English Language.

## Carleton enacts Quebec Act after French fail at memorizing every inbred British monarch

GLORIOUS AND/OR FREE | 32

—— JUNE 22, 1774 ——

QUEBEC CITY — Governor Guy Carleton has given up on formally assimilating the French race and has passed an Act restoring Catholic rights and French civil law. The frustrated Governor made the decision when the class he himself was teaching was unable to memorize each incestuous royal marriage involving the English.

Claiming that the French race had to reach an established standard at becoming English, Carleton decreed that the French showed a genuine disinterest in becoming properly civilized with the knowledge of royal inbreeding.

"Every time I asked my class which cousin Queen Mary I married, I get a blank stare from the whole lot of them," lamented Carlton in front of a family tree diagram. "Well, it was pretty obvious: her first cousin once removed, Phillip II of Spain."

The class was reportedly clueless on the marriages of Edward I, Richard III, and William III to their cousins, despite Carleton's clear guidance.

"These people will never be British," added Carleton, who also expanded the borders of Quebec so he could stay as far away from what he called the "Creton-munching brutes."

# A Dear John Adams Letter

—— SEPTEMBER 10, 1774 ——

*Having spent years as trading partners of the Americans, it was just sort of assumed that the Atlantic colonies would join the fledgling Revolution after the battles of Lexington and Concord. However, the provinces all eventually refused the American request. Below is a letter from Nova Scotia aristocrat Geoff Fletcher to John Adams of Massachusetts explaining why they wouldn't be taking part.*

—

My dearest John,

I received your report on English effrontery in your state and others with great concern. Truly the armies of George III have stained the honour of their mother country with their conduct. The destruction of businesses and the persecution of women and children you detailed induced my eyes to wet and my hands to tremble. Know that your cause is in my prayers every night.

You also mentioned your surprise that we, the people of Nova Scotia, had yet to rise up with you. To, as you say, "throw off the yoke of our shared colonial oppressors. To do battle with our sovereign so that we may emerge from the fire and blood of war as free men, beholden to no one but a government of our own choosing!"

So yeah, about that. I've been meaning to get back to you—things have just been super crazy lately. Unfortunately, it doesn't look like we're going to be able to make it to the Revolution. Don't get me wrong, it sounds like a ton of fun. We just have a lot going on right now.

For starters, we like, just got an elected assembly. It doesn't even have any power yet and we still can't seem to figure out how to make it work. I don't really want to think about what it would be like if a "government, by and for the people" were to try to operate out of there.

Also, don't know if you know this, but a lot of British soldiers are quartered in Halifax. They spend a lot of money here, actually. Frankly, they're keeping the place afloat. And if we joined you guys it would be less "Let's go out for a pint and tip well" and a lot more "Everybody's dead!" Can't swing it, I'm afraid.

Finally, I'm thinking about going back to school in the fall, so I just won't have time.

I hope my letter does not displease you too greatly. I'm sure the Revolution will still be great without us. Better, even.

See you at Christmas.

    Love,

        Geoff

---

### IN THE NEWS

Mad King George attempts to sell PEI to Mongolia

---

Canadian militia encouraged to point in same direction at next battle

## Canada's Declaration of Dependence — July 5, 1776

*Showing their unflinching loyalty to King and Country, many Canadians signed up to declare themselves entirely dependent on Britain, promising never to depart the mother country. Here's that response to the American Declaration of Independence, signed a day after the American decree.*

JULY 5, 1776.

### The unanimous Declaration of Dependence on Great Britain from the Well-Behaved Colonies of Canada

When in the course of history, a Righteous Royal is threatened by a treasonous colonial revolt motivated by repugnant republicanism and the foreign idea of democracy, loyal subjects must answer the call of our dependency. —— We hold these principles to be self-evident that all men are subjects of the King of Great Britain no matter how many times he may be rude or doesn't return our letters. He is a WISE AND benevolent Sovereign whom we rely on for such things as Decrees, Edicts, Laws, and other forms of instruction. —— The people would be lost without him.

Perpetual consent to do whatever.

Unflinching loyalty, taxation without representation or self-determination.

Duty to remain silent, and just go with it.

We invite British troops to quarter with us, make themselves feel welcome, and enjoy our womenfolk.

God Save the King!

# A Loyalist Reflects

———— MARCH 29, 1783 ————

*A staunch believer in the monarchy and the British Empire, Loyalist Henry Morneau moved to Canada from New York in 1783 after being attacked by his countrymen for refusing to support the new republic. His diary entry, recorded only a few days after his arrival, shows a man still uncertain about his choice.*

—

I fucked up. I fucked up real bad.

What was I thinking? Sure I was a fan of King George and British rule, but mostly I just thought crowns were awesome. When everyone around me started losing their minds ranting about "republicanism" I decided to stand up and voice my disagreement. But I was just playing devil's advocate! I thought Jennifer the butcher's daughter would like me more if she saw that I'd defend my ideals and refuse to simply go along with what's popular. But then she dumped me for that French motherfucker Lafayette!

I had no idea the Americans would actually win! I figured the British troops would roll over them. Then maybe they would have given me an award for loyalty, like making me mayor or giving me a pig. But nope! I had to run out of town with my tail between my legs or else they would have tarred and feathered me like they did Keith, the guy who tried to make a schedule for quartering soldiers in private homes.

And now I'm here. Stuck in this backwater country full of Indians and guys who sound a lot like Lafayette. It's only been a few days and I already know I hate it here. Where is the culture? Where is the community? Where is the person who picks up horse shit from the streets so you don't have to spend all day looking down to avoid it?

I remember my very first day here. I was exhausted, freezing cold, and up to my knees in manure because I hadn't yet learned the "look down" system. I stumbled into a tavern and ordered the daily special from the barman. I cannot accurately describe the quality of the meal he brought me except to say I would have been better off eating the leftover feathers they didn't use on Keith.

What do people even do here? Every single person I've met works in furs. Fur trader, fur salesman, accountant who specializes in fur taxes. I have a feeling my experience as a librarian isn't going to help much.

I am devastated, but not broken. I'm sure it's just a matter of time until Americans calm down about this whole Revolution thing and begin welcoming people like me back home. But for now I have to go. My new neighbour is insisting I attend something called a "cricket match" with him.

## Loyalist fleeing oppression, abuse brings slave with him to Canada

———— APRIL 4, 1784 ————

KINGSTON — Hero of the Empire Eli Carter has arrived in Canada after fleeing the terrible persecution American colonists are inflicting on those who remained loyal to their king during the recent "troubles." He has arrived with only a few possessions: his clothes, his rifle, and his personal slave, Malcolm.

"The cruelty my former neighbours showed themselves capable of was beyond imagination," said Carter as he affixed the chain to Malcolm's neck. "I mean, tarring and feathering? Haven't we moved beyond that as a species?

"I'm just so grateful that here I can be accepted for exactly who I am and what I do. I literally didn't have to change a thing when I entered the country."

Carter's terrifying journey to freedom required him to leave in the middle of the night, taking with him only what Malcolm could carry. Numerous treasured belongings, like his coin collection and Malcolm's wife, had to be left behind.

"I'm sure it will take a while for Eli to adjust to life here," said new neighbour Elizabeth Moore. "He won't be able to use his slave to grow cotton because it's too cold for the crop, but the important thing is he'll be safe, and still able to keep his slave."

Malcolm was available for comment, but we felt no need to ask him anything.

# Fur trader tired of having to walk through perfume section of Hudson's Bay Company

———— AUGUST 30, 1785 ————

MONTREAL – Hudson's Bay fur trader Robert Cloutier has expressed his displeasure of having to walk through the perfume and beauty section every time he visits the store to drop off a load of furs.

"My nose tingles every time I walk by the kiosks," explained Cloutier carrying a 50-pound pack of beaver pelts. "Dozens of workers try to sell me some Eau de Pin or Eau de King George. Sometimes they just spray it in my face without asking, which causes me to sneeze uncontrollably. Don't they know I have a fragrance allergy?"

"I'm just hear to unload some dead animal skins."

HBC is trying to diversify beyond fur trading by selling more high-end goods like perfume, pearls, and silk long johns. It's all part of the company's new slogan: Hudson's Bay Company—fewer bloody furs, more fun blankets.

According to sources, Cloutier became lost in the children's pantaloon and butter churning section on his way to the fur depot.

**HUDSON'S BAY COMPANY**

*"fewer bloody furs, more fun blankets."*

# Governor Simcoe decrees new August long weekend for slaves

———— JULY 10, 1793 ————

YORK — To celebrate the nearly end of slavery in Upper Canada, Governor John Graves Simcoe has given those who'll still be slaves a long weekend in August.

"All those who will remain a slave for the rest of their lives, and any children of slaves born hereafter who will be slaves until age 25, will need a day off," declared Simcoe. "During that time, the slaves can appreciate how humane and Christian it was of me to prohibit the importation of slavery to Upper Canada. They should be proud knowing that their race has been emancipated, freed from the burden as they carry on with their duties that they are obliged to do."

Six out of the 16 members of the Executive Council who own slaves say they'll be especially nice to their human property during that weekend.

# Spoilsport magistrate bans duelling

———— JANUARY 17, 1800 ————

NEWARK, UPPER CANADA — A no-fun judge in Upper Canada has decreed all duelling, even the gentlemanly kind, illegal from this day forth.

Malcontented magistrate Thomas Brent Thimbleby grumbled that anyone participating in a duel would be punished under criminal law. His sourpuss statement comes a fortnight after Mr. John White and Mr. John Small engaged in a playful bit of sport that resulted in Mr. White's death.

"While duels can be entertaining to watch, someone may get hurt," moaned Thimbleby. "Men can resolve their disputes, no matter how big or small, through other, more reasonable mechanisms. We need not kill each other over things that can be resolved peacefully."

All weaponry, from cannon, musket, and pistols to swords, maces, and sticks, has been banned by the wet blanket in robes. The ruling has disappointed many in the duelling community.

"How can m'lud disqualify a strong English tradition?" asked Harold Percy, president of the Upper Canada Gentleman Duelling Society. "This will surely hurt our recruitment. We already lose half our members each year."

## The Upper Crust of Upper Canada

As Loyalists and other anglophones settled into the parts of Canada that would one day become Ontario, the province quickly developed a hierarchical class structure similar to that of England. At the top were a group of wealthy merchants and government elite who came to be known as the Family Compact. These aristocrats dominated public life in the colony. Among the most prominent families were the Davenports. Below is a family tree commissioned by patriarch Roland Davenport in 1835.

A fairly typical family tree showing four generations of Davenports. Roland and his wife, Clarissa, are at the top. But in subsequent generations the lines clearly show people breeding with their cousins.

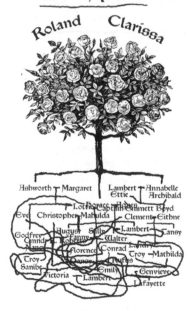

# THE WAR OF 1812 (THROUGH 1815)

*Fresh off its victorious Revolution and feeling like a big strong man, America didn't waste much time before turning its attention to expansion. The war it brought about by invading its northern neighbour would see Canadians fighting honourably to defend their soil, repelling the aggressors and giving the country the kind of quasi-military victory that we all collectively agreed was good enough.*

# Diddle-Diddle-Dumpling War renamed War of 1812

———— AUGUST 19, 1812 ————

LONDON — His Majesty King George III has decreed that the ongoing conflict with the United States will no longer be called the Diddle-Diddle-Dumpling War but rather the War of 1812. The king's trusted advisers encouraged him to change the name after many of the generals who had overheard the moniker for the struggle in North America responded with "My Son John" in a most childish manner. This is not the first time His Majesty has changed the name of particular conflicts throughout the globe. Last year he renamed the Pat-a-Cake, Pat-a-Cake, Baker's Man War as the Peninsular War. In addition, what is now known as the Gunboat War was previously known as a series of whoops and hollers.

# Heroic Canadian militia defeat American army through grit, determination, overwhelming British military support

——— OCTOBER 13, 1812 ———

QUEENSTON HEIGHTS — Armed only with their own courage and the backing of thousands of well-trained British troops, Canadian militia forces dealt a devastating blow to the American army at the Battle of Queenston Heights.

"The Americans were simply no match for our pluck," said militia leader Tommy Kaplan. "That, and I guess Isaac Brock's mortars helped a little."

Kaplan then turned and yelled "We did it, boys!" at the hundred or so lightly armed militiamen who had participated in the battle.

Military experts are already praising the Canadians' tactic of following British orders to stay in the reserve, noting that it was likely what turned the tide of the battle—as opposed to the actual tide washing a number of American ships downstream, preventing their soldiers from landing.

"We lost a lot of good men. Jack got shot in the arm. Mark got spooked and ran away. Terrible tragedies," said Kaplan as British soldiers dug a grave for their dozens of dead.

The Canadian warriors added that they know the fighting isn't over. They're already making plans to tell everyone that they helped burn down the White House.

## America's War Strategy

*In the run-up to their invasion, America's generals drafted the following battle plan. As you'll see, the plan indicates that the United States thought conquering Canada would be no great challenge.*

—

## TACTICAL PLAN FOR THE INVASION OF BRITISH NORTH AMERICA

**STEP ONE:**
Assemble men. Ideally 10,000, but 20–30 will probably do it.

**STEP TWO:**
Walk toward border.

**STEP THREE:**
Cross border with men.

**STEP FOUR:**
Advise locals that they've been conquered.

**STEP FIVE:**
Organize victory parade.

# General Brock's dying words: "Name a mediocre university after me"

———— OCTOBER 13, 1812 ————

QUEENSTON — With the Yankee foes vanquished from the battlefield of Queenston, our mortally wounded hero, Major General Sir Isaac Brock, uttered his final words.

Clutching one of the men of the 49th Foot, the general—who had captured Fort Detroit, negotiated an alliance with the Mohawks, and oversaw the defence of Canada from American invasion—tried to inspire his men by proclaiming that one day their descendants may attend the local university in the event that they're not accepted elsewhere.

"Push on, brave volunteers," a wounded Brock said before collapsing. "And make the school's mascot some type of . . . aggressive . . . carnivorous . . . ferret."

Major General Roger Hale Sheaffe, who gallantly repulsed the Yankee invaders with an organized counterattack, vowed he would persevere in order to ensure that young minds would always have at least one fallback option.

"Whilst Major General Brock's own counterattack was ultimately unsuccessful, I will not rest until we regain the Heights and also have some place to send our third-rate students after high school," said Scheaffe.

# Heroic chocolatier Laura Secord defeats American forces with type 2 diabetes

———— JUNE 20, 1813 ————

BEAVER DAM, UPPER CANADA — The prolonged American occupation of the Niagara Frontier ended last night after the majority of U.S. troops withdrew, thanks to the many sugar-rich, nutrient-poor chocolates served to them by loyal British subject Laura Secord.

"I have no feeling in my right foot," moaned a retreating and overweight Private Elazer Pendleton Gaines of the 21st U.S. Infantry Regiment. "Curses be that wicked trollop and her Milk Chocolate Almond Swirls! Damn the British!"

General Jacob Brown was also reportedly poisoned by the heroine after she used her sly wit to secrete walnuts into his Crinkle Cup, knowing full well that the U.S. commander had a nut allergy.

# You Are Invited to David Thompson's Birthday Party

*Here's a detailed map.*

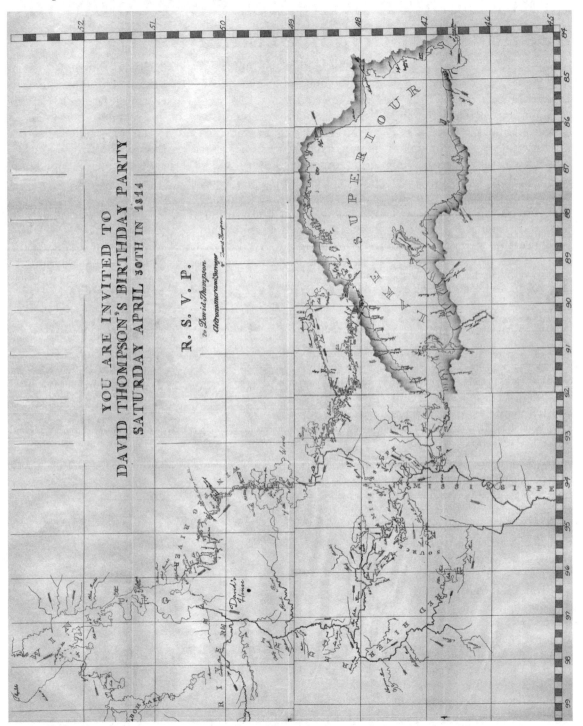

# But it's a dry cold: Letter from Mrs. Lacey Erin Maclaren in the Red River Colony to her mother, Ethyl, in Scotland

—— FEBRUARY 16, 1813 ——

Dearest Mother,

Thank you for your letter and concerns about my perishing in a frosty hellscape. Although I may have lost my dearest John when he froze to death after a few moments exposed to the outdoors, and although the land lacks the most basic of necessities due to the icy climate, I must emphasize that the coldness here is better because it is "dry." Yes, a dry cold.

You may not understand this as you are used to the wet colds in Aberdeen, which are worse. And, sure, the blustery winds may split open my lips like an axe to a tree trunk, and you may not have all your limbs amputated from frostbite, but I am truly embracing this unique kind of temperature. The icicles that hang from my nostrils sparkle in the crisp air. The cold doesn't seep into my clothes as it has already chilled down to the bone. The frost-encrusted beards of the men are not damp; they are frozen solid. Please send for more settlers.

Your always loving daughter,

Lacey

---

# HBC–North West Company merger settles dispute over Canada's last beaver pelt

—— JULY 7, 1821 ——

MONTREAL — The two giants of the fur trade industry in British North America have finalized their business merger, putting an end to 40 years of intense rivalry.

"After decades of ravaging the beaver population, we decided that the time was right to merge," said HBC president George Simpson. "Otherwise, we'll spend the next 30 years fighting over who'll get to sell the last pelt."

Given their representatives' deep-seated, mutual hatred, a merger between these two corporations would have seemed impossible just a few years ago. In 1816 the tension boiled over into direct conflict during the battle of Seven Oaks—a giant tug-of-war over two beaver pelts

Fur trader contemplating whether dog pelts would make nice coats.

that ended in the furs ripping down the middle. This ruinous result sparked violence that left 21 recorded dead and one with hurt feelings.

Simpson went on to announce that the new HBC would focus its business mainly on tote bags and women's undergarments.

## The Family Compact's Rude Report

*"Family Compact" was the term given to the political elite who ruled Upper Canada from the end of the War of 1812 through to 1837. They regularly issued the Rude Report in a catty effort to shame those who did not comply with proper colonial conduct. They also issued scathing punishments. The following artifact is a PSA, issued through* The Beaverton, *c. 1825.*

# PROCLAMATION.
### in the form of
# THE RUDE REPORT

*Fellow citizens,*

The following individuals have made slights and errors against our established colonial code of conduct:

**MR. WENDELL SMITH OF YORK** used a soup spoon instead of a dinner spoon at Mr. and Mrs. Carl Hopper's dinner party, creating quite a scene and much embarrassment for the other guests trying to maintain some sense of decency and civilization in this otherwise barren land. Such savagery will not be tolerated.

### Punishment
*Banishment from the colony.*

**MR. ALAN DAVID MOODY OF BYTOWN** briefly conversed with a known Irishman while walking to his law offices without scorning him for his perverse belief in popery and failing to deliver a swift kick in the Irishman's behind causing him to fall in a mud puddle. Mr. Moody's lack of complicity in honouring our sacred Irish-kicking is an affront to Protestant morals and the manner in which we properly govern ourselves.

### Punishment
*A nasty rumour shall be started about Mr. Moody's wife and her gardening abilities.*

While discoursing during a dinner party with Mr. Henry Sherwood of Brockville, **MR. HENRY FISCHER OF KINGSTON** spoke rather too succinctly with regard to the politically sensitive issue of the Welland Canal's ongoing construction. Mr. Fischer boorishly uttered "It's coming along, eh?" to Mr. Sherwood, who was notably disturbed for the rest of the evening by this lowbrow outburst that butchered the King's English.

### Punishment
*Not being invited to high tea this Sunday.
Also, one month in the stocks.*

**THE HATHAWAY FAMILY OF LENNOX COUNTY** arrived at St. James Anglican Church two minutes late, interrupting the opening hymn and attracting a sharp glare from Reverend Alexander MacDonald. Mr. John Hathaway later apologized for his family's lack of social graces and respect for the Lord Almighty and the Reverend by claiming their tardiness was owing to his need to bury their infant son that same morning. However, this farmer of lowly crops that feed on the vilest dirt had already used that excuse for their previous infant son.

### Punishment
*No one in the colony shall ever look a member of the Hathaway family (including descendants) in the eye again.*

**MR. DANIEL WIGGINS OF COBOURG**, lacking in patriotic comportment and duty to his sovereign, failed to start and end his sentence with "God Save the King" when addressing Sir Allan Napier, 1st Baronet of the Legislature of Upper Canada, while attending a cricket match last week. This rather crass implication of Upper Canada's having achieved independence reeks of Yankee Republicanism and verges on treason and treachery.

### Punishment
*Flogging and memorization of the entire royal family, including the king's Habsburgian second cousins and their mistresses.*

Bishop John Strachan, FAMILY COMPACT member in goodstanding.

# Lost birds of Labrador, 1833

*American ornithologist John James Audubon visited the Labrador coast to document bird species, some of which are now extinct. Here are his sketches of three of these fascinating creatures.*

*Chicken-winged warbler.*

*Red-headed Knot Crane.*

*Crianius gigantigus Passeridae.*

# Colonel By pleased to announce completion of longest skating rink

———— MAY 29, 1832 ————

BYTOWN — After six years of construction, £822,804, and approximately 1000 worker casualties, Upper Canada's longest skating rink has been completed.

"I hope you will take pride in knowing the vastness of your contribution to Canada," By said to his workers. "Through your sacrifice you have created a tourist attraction. And not just any tourist attraction, but a pretty fun tourist attraction."

The project was initiated after government officials determined that they had no way to safely transport laughing children and couples on a first date from the St. Lawrence to the rest of Upper Canada.

"It's also going to be great for the thousands of people who will soon be forced to live and work here," added By.

When asked what the skating rink would be used for during summers, By shrugged and said, "I guess you could boat down it or something."

# Neighbours outraged by proposed two-storey building in downtown Toronto

—— NOVEMBER 29, 1834 ——

TORONTO — Indignant citizens of the newly renamed Toronto were annoyed to hear that the Mackenzie family had plans to build a towering two-storey building, a structure that will surely cast a long shadow and obscure the views of many nearby residences.

Construction of the six-room house on Yonge Street is set to begin next month, yet many locals have petitioned City Council and Mayor Robert Sullivan to put an immediate halt to the site now dubbed Toronto's Tower of Babylon.

One resident, Caleb John Chadwick of #24 Spadina, who has dwelled in the city for the past 12 years, said the monstrous building will obscure his Lake Ontario and brick factory vista.

"My shack has a wonderful view of those smokestacks and the horizon. I purchased the property for £3, 15 shillings, but now with the proposed tower, it may not even be worth £2."

In response to the outcry, Mayor Sullivan has reassured the populace that none of the rooms in the massive structure would be sold or rented to an Irishman.

# THE
# BEAVER  TOWN.

PUBLISHED SIMULTANEOUSLY                    IN HALIFAX AND TORONTO.

### Trusted Journal of News, Politics, Rhetoric & Industry.

*$4 per annum.* — FRIDAY DECEMBER 8, 1837 — *payable in advance.*

*W.L. Mackenzie.*

### TORONTO PUB CRAWL MISTAKEN FOR REBELLION AGAINST CROWN

Chaos broke out on Yonge Street yesterday evening after a drunken trek to many of the city's pubs was misinterpreted as an open rebellion against His Majesty's government in an effort to secure the province's independence and turn it into a republic.

"Oh no, we were just having a bit of a boys' night out," said alleged rebellion leader/head party planner William Lyon Mackenzie. "You know that classic drinking game where you get together with 400 of your best friends and some of you have muskets?

"I mean, a few hundred men wandering aimlessly around pubs—who would ever call that a rebellion?"

Nerves have been on edge in the colony, with government officials and Family Compact members worrying that radicals might emulate the revolt that broke out in Lower Canada last month. Accordingly, 15,000 armed soldiers were sent to disperse Mackenzie's group just as their "Never Have I Ever" game was heating up.

"In retrospect, maybe we overreacted a little," said Colonel James FitzGibbon, the man charged with defeating the rebellion forces. "But at least by engaging these drunks in a late-night shootout on the street we sobered them up enough that they could safely carriage home."

At press time, a game of Flip Cup was being arranged to determine which of the rebels would be hanged.

### QUEBEC'S ENGLISH RULERS BREAK SEVERAL MONOCLES UPON HEARING OF FRENCH REVOLT

In Montreal, members of the elite Chateau Clique have broken twelve monocles after receiving word that British forces were defeated at St-Denis by Les Patriotes.

"Oh my!" exclaimed Jonathan Sewell, who cracked his gold-rimmed monocle earlier this week. "This news is quite disturbing. This just goes to show the French race does not deserve to govern themselves and we should continue to be their rulers."

News of the rebellion has caused great shock and worry among the astonished gentlemen's family members, who gasped while holding their hands over their mouths and domestic servants who let go of fine chinaware they were holding.

"My wife is so worried. She has clutched her pearls twice this week," remarked John Stewart, Esq. to his Executive Council colleagues. "When I heard Jean-Louis Papineau was part of this, I nearly spilled my cognac. That devil!"

# REBELLION STRUGGLE & Mutton Chops
## (1837–1867)

"I expected to find a conflict between the government and its people. Instead I found two nations having a sexy pillow fight in the bosom of a single state." —Report of Lord Durham, 1839

As the midpoint of the 19th century dawned, Britain maintained its tenuous control over France Two. In Ontario the descendants of British loyalists were ruled by the stern Family Compact regime. And in the Maritimes there were probably some things happening too. But these three regions, to date so independent in their trajectories, were about to be united by the sheer drunken force of John A. Macdonald. Through his courage and conviction, Canada would become the semi-independent legal dominion under a British monarch that we all know and love.

# KEY DATES

**November 6, 1837**
French rebellion fails due to
money and the ethnic vote

**January 5, 1838**
Third Rebellion in Maritimes just
four guys out for a walk

**February 11, 1839**
Lord Durham recommends that the
provinces of Upper and Lower Canada
be combined into one province
named Super Awesome Fun Place

**February 10, 1841**
Britain forces Upper and Lower
Canada to share a room

**April 12, 1861**
U.S. Civil War breaks out, temporarily
distracting Americans from their
constant plans to invade Canada

**July 1, 1867**
Tragically Hip play first-ever Canada Day

# RESPONSIBLE REBELLION

*Shockingly, the British conquering Quebec and trying to impose English Protestant values on a French Catholic population, then bringing in thousands of English speakers to settle what would become Ontario, created some friction. In both provinces, reformers began to agitate against the colonial governments, which consisted of the governor general and whatever small dogs he happened to breed. When agitation grew into rebellion, Britain had no choice but to turn to John George Lambton, or, as he was known on the street, Lord Durham. Sure, Durham had been retired ever since his wife died during his last mission. But he agreed to come back for one last ride.*

# Reform Campaign Ribbons

*Much like their American counterparts during their campaign for independence, Upper Canadian reformers relied on pithy catchphrases like the one below to drum up support for the idea of Responsible Government.*

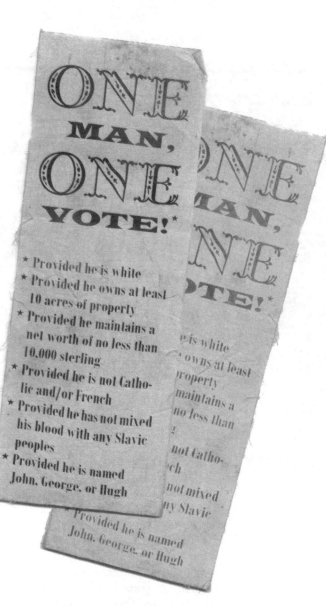

ONE MAN, ONE VOTE!

* Provided he is white
* Provided he owns at least 10 acres of property
* Provided he maintains a net worth of no less than 10,000 sterling
* Provided he is not Catholic and/or French
* Provided he has not mixed his blood with any Slavic peoples
* Provided he is named John, George, or Hugh

# Second draft of The Durham Report

*The Durham Report of 1839 had a permanent impact on the nation's development; its plan to merge the legislatures of Upper and Lower Canada laid the very groundwork for Confederation. Although not enacted for some time, the Report also called for "Responsible Government"—an executive authority that could govern only with the consent and approval of the elected legislature. However, this bit wasn't always part of the Report, as you can see from this early draft.*

—

LORD DURHAM'S REPORT ON THE AFFAIRS OF BRITISH NORTH AMERICA (DRAFT 2)

Your Majesty,

I present to you my findings of the causes of the Rebellions of 1837–1838 in Upper and Lower Canada. Please accept this initial summary of recommendations to improve the overall state and well-being of the colonies in Canada:

~~Kill the French bastards~~ Establish responsible government.

~~Wipe their seed from the earth and destroy any symbol of the French Canadien~~ Combine the Upper Canada and Lower Canada legislatures to ease Upper Canada's debt load and exploit Lower Canada's surplus.

~~Mass starvation~~ Govern according to the principles of peace, order and good government.

~~Assimilate survivors~~ Rescind the freedoms of the Royal Proclamation of 1763 and the Quebec Act of 1774.

~~Kill assimilated survivors~~ Create municipal governments.

## PUBLIC NOTICE,
by

WILLIAM LYON MACKENZIE

### Re: Overthrow of Upper Canada's Government, Refreshments

DECEMBER 7, 1837

If anyone is interested in overthrowing the government to establish a Republic, please meet at Montgomery Tavern on December 7 at 12 p.m. Bring your own gun/pitchfork. Refrain from telling the current authorities, as this event is

## SECRET.

Refreshments will follow after declaration of victory.

# Rebellion vet asks if thing they fought and died for can have better name than Responsible Government

—— OCTOBER 27, 1839 ——

MONTREAL — In a desperate plea, 1837 Rebellion veteran Louis Laporte has requested that the major reform he and his companions fought and, in many cases, died for could be given a "cooler title" than Responsible Government.

"Don't get me wrong, I'm in favour of making the executive accountable to the legislature," said Laporte. "It's just 'Responsible Government' sounds like something a substitute teacher came up with during civics class.

"Couldn't we call it 'democracy' or maybe 'Awesome Government Big-Time Action'?"

Laporte, who took on a squad of British soldiers almost by himself, is just one of many frustrated that their heroic actions will forever be tied to a name that sounds about as exciting as a Sunday stroll through the park.

These men have been exasperated by similar "boring name" habits throughout the country, including calling the provinces just Canada West and Canada East and naming every hotel the Prince of Wales.

# Politician wins election after sending clear "bat-to-face" message to voters

—— FEBRUARY 22, 1841 ——

MIDDLESEX, CANADA WEST — Conservative member Edward Ermatinger has won in a landslide after he and his burly re-election team won 99% of the votes in the riding of Middlesex, using his practised skills of persuasion aided by several bats to the face.

His bloodied Reform opponent, Victor McKnight, mustered only three votes, all of which were disqualified after election officials determined that those individuals either did not own property or were assumed to be women disguised as men.

"I would like to extend a heartfelt thanks to all of you who shouted my name without any encouragement from my loyal goons," announced Mr. Ermatinger from the hustings with McKnight seated beside him, unconscious and bleeding from his nose. "It has become apparent that this constituency needs a strong, powerful voice with an equally strong bat swing."

Mr. Ermatinger's promises included 12 ounces of whisky in every stomach, a new railway that runs directly to a railway baron's estate, and fewer Catholics.

Eyewitnesses called the election a remarkable demonstration of democracy, as many of Ermatinger's supporters were able to vote on behalf of those who'd met some unfortunate circumstances involving injury and were unable to make the poll. Turnout was up from the previous election, with 454% of all registered voters casting a ballot.

# LIFE IN 19TH-CENTURY CANADA

*Outside of what was known in Britain as "those cute little rebellions of 1837," life in the United Province of Canada as well as in Nova Scotia, PEI, New Brunswick, and Newfoundland* *appeared to be relatively tranquil in the mid-19th century. But underneath this calm exterior lay the boiling hot bloodlust Canadians would become known for.*

## Emigration Bulletin

*In the 19th century, Britain encouraged thousands of citizens to move to the colony in exchange for the promise of land. These new colonists were warned of a few differences between life at home and life in the New World.*

—

## Franklin expedition sets sail for Northwest Passage with 128 delicious-looking crew members

——— MAY 19, 1845 ———

GREENHITHE, ENGLAND — Sir John Franklin, captain and expert navigator, set a course for the Northwest Passage in two ships fully supplied with healthy, scrumptious Royal Navy sailors.

"I'm very pleased I was able to find such high-quality, seasoned sailors," declared Captain Franklin, licking his lips before setting sail. "All of you are truly the spine, muscles, and succulent thighs of this ship. I am depending on you to keep me and some of the less-appetizing officers alive as we make this arduous journey across the frigid Canadian Arctic."

Franklin wisely instructed his men to fatten up before setting sail by consuming solid blocks of butter, lard, and "as much vittles as possible" to endure the harsh wind, ice, and snow.

However, Franklin made it quite clear that he'd be running a tight ship, outlining that punishments for any misbehaviour would include roasting in a pot for 8–10 minutes per pound.

The crew is hoping that naming one of their ships HMS *Terror* and the other HMS *Erebus*—after a Greek demigod that guards the gates of hell—will give them great luck in returning safe and uneaten.

## Things to Know BEFORE Emigrating to CANADA

*Canada does not have a class system. The only thing that distinguishes the common labourer from the wealthy merchant is the overwhelming difference in quality of life.*

**You will need to learn how to say "Please don't kill me" in French and a dozen Native languages.**

**They say "cunt" slightly less than we do.**

**All the men are named Steve.**

**They don't know we're planning to sell them to the Americans. DO NOT TELL THEM.**

## Johnson brothers' execution sets new attendance record

———— OCTOBER 22, 1847 ————

YORK — The hanging of famous bank robbers Ernie and Windermere Johnson saw the highest turnout yet for public executions in Upper Canada.

"We knew this would draw a crowd, especially after Windermere threatened to kill the judge at his trial," said Archibald Simpson, commissioner of the Death Penalty League. "But no one thought we'd outperform last fall when we hanged Jimmy the Kid.

"It just goes to show how much people like watching other people die," he added.

Residents flocked by the thousands to the square, leaving school classrooms empty, factory machines stalled, and pigs temporarily unbutchered. Fathers put their children on their shoulders to get a better view. Vendors were sold out of candy corn and official execution programs almost immediately.

"Unfortunately, I didn't have a great view of Windermere, but I locked eyes with Ernie right as his neck snapped. My friends are going to be so jealous," exclaimed Bertrun Weston, 14.

For his part, Simpson said the joy he saw in the faces of all those gathered was what public executions were about.

"Sure, we made some money off the event. But, as an organization, what truly matters to us is bringing people together."

## Hudson's Bay Company unveils own version of Responsible Government: GIVE US YOUR FUCKING FURS

———— MAY 14, 1848 ————

RUPERT'S LAND — The administration of the Hudson Bay Company, which has dominion over all land west of the Canadian province, has recently implemented its own version of Responsible Government. They call it "Hand Over Your Goddamn Furs or We'll Shoot."

"Our new legislative style is quite similar to what you've implemented in Ontario and Quebec," said HBC administrator Percy Winterbottom. "Only instead of the executive needing the support of the legislature, our system requires the executive to get all the fucking furs in anyone's possession at all times, or else we start fucking your shit up.

"Otherwise, it's pretty much identical."

The reform, having passed the board of directors' vote unanimously, will immediately take effect for fur traders employed by HBC as well as the thousands of Métis and Aboriginals who happen to live in the area arbitrarily awarded to the company.

"We hope this move will vanquish any doubts that we're not sympathetic to the concerns of our indentured servants . . . I mean citizens," said Winterbottom.

Under the system, residents will have "until the count of three" to turn over their furs. Those who don't will face the "our foot up your ass" and/or the "our hand down your throat" penalty.

Before adopting the Canadian system, HBC did consider an American-inspired governance style, with three separate fur-taking authorities acting as a check and balance on each other as they take your furs.

# Woman perfects blank expression

———— MAY 4, 1847 ————

KINGSTON — After years of struggling to prevent disgust and disbelief from overrunning her face during genteel dinner table discussions, Mrs. James Gale Ferris, formerly known as Caroline Jeffery, has mastered the impassive countenance.

"We were eating dinner and my husband expressed the belief that too much reading causes hysteria in women," said friend Mrs. Heather Devonshire.

"Caroline didn't even move a muscle. It was amazing."

After much practice, Mrs. Ferris has been able to stop her eyes from automatically rolling every time men give their opinion on gender, politics, or society at large. The only betrayal of her internal thoughts at the dinner was a slight downturn of her lower lip, which (with admirable skill) Ferris masked with a quick dab of her napkin.

Mrs. Jane Robinson, who runs a prestigious academy for women and girls in Toronto, said that women must cultivate this technique in order to survive the rigours of contemporary intellectual conversation.

"Many women find they involuntarily twitch or convulse when listening to rational masculine topics, such as the necessity of having mistresses. This is because our minds and constitutions are weaker," Mrs. Robinson explained.

Mrs. Ferris credits her ability to years of, training, rehearsal, and focusing on the wallpaper.

## Tories deny burning down Parliament despite "Burn Parliament Down" slogan

———— APRIL 25, 1849 ————

MONTREAL — Conservative members of what was the Legislature of Canada insisted they had absolutely nothing to do with the mob that set the Parliament buildings ablaze despite their new "Burn Parliament Down" campaign motto.

"It's merely a figure of speech," said Tory member William Henry Boulton to the press while holding a torch. "We were simply expressing our frustration at the government's compensating those treasonous Patriots for their 1837 Rebellion losses. No one would take what

we said literally."

Boulton further clarified that he and his party are stumped as to who would encourage a mass of people to pelt the governor general with rotten vegetables and foul eggs.

"We have no idea why they did that," exclaimed Conservative

member John Wilson. "But it was probably the French, those no-good, tourtière-munching guttersnipes. We should burn down Quebec!

"Burn Quebec! Burn Quebec!" he chanted before reminding everyone not to take his words out of context.

# 1850 Fashion: New line of dresses blend women in with wallpaper

# Underground Railroad allows black man to escape to country where he can't vote or send kids to school

———— NOVEMBER 27, 1851 ————

WINDSOR, CANADA WEST — After months of treacherous journeying to Canada West, former slave William Freemen is now able to experience the liberty that comes with living in a place where you cannot participate in the democratic process or enrol your children in public education.

"I am so grateful to have made it across the border into Canada," said Freemen. "I'm no longer a slave to a master. Instead, I'm in a legal grey area where I can own property but not participate in my own governance or send my children to a province-run school.

"But I still have to pay tax!" he added.

Freemen is just one of thousands of slaves who cut the chains of their own bondage and travelled north in order to experience the not-quite-as-bad-as-America racism of the British colonies. Previously arrived residents like Abigail Watson said the risk was well worth it.

"I refused to spend another day under the threat of a whip. Now I only have to deal with shopkeepers refusing me entry to their stores, people crossing the street to avoid me, and mobs coming to kill me should I marry a white man."

# Moodie's book *I Hate Canada* praised by Canadians

——— JULY 17, 1852 ———

BELLEVILLE, CANADA WEST — Critics and readers everywhere, from London, England, to rural Canada, are raving about Susanna Moodie's newest tract, appropriately called *I Hate Canada: Why You Should Never Move Here*, published earlier this year.

Moodie brilliantly taps into the common thread of disgust felt by most, if not all, British immigrants newly settled in Canada. As she explains in the foreword, "I was always taught to write from the heart, and my heart tells me this so-called land of opportunity is absolutely wretched."

Many readers are bonding over the shared experience of hating where they live. Take, for example, Mrs. Jonathan Markem: "Before reading Moodie, I thought I was the only one who loathed the endless trees, the proximity of raucous, licentious Yankees, and the horrible stench of Irish immigrants. Now, not only do I feel closer to my fellow displaced British citizens in this destitute wilderness, I also have a growing sense of what it means, dare I say it, to be a Canadian."

Moodie's articulation of a Canadian identity founded on a sense of self-loathing has not discouraged new immigrants from Britain. On the contrary, her tirade against the oppressively dark nights, the settlers' battle to clear thick forests, and the dispiriting lack of street-corner tea houses has only put fire to the flame of British settlement in the Province of Canada.

"The success of British colonization relies on the British tendency to flock where they will be least happy," explained Immigration Minister George Keenon. "I believe it is the Protestant work impulse. Susanna Moodie's book has been such an effective tool that we're considering replacing all our promotional material with it."

# Macdonald government falls after he shows up at Parliament sober

——— JULY 28, 1858 ———

QUEBEC CITY — The government of John A. Macdonald collapsed this morning after a scandalous affair in which the colony's premier arrived in Parliament without any traces of alcohol in his system whatsoever.

> "This is outrageous! . . . This teetotaller across from me is not the man the people chose to lead them," said Opposition leader George Brown

"This is outrageous!" hollered Opposition leader George Brown from the front row. "Do you mean to tell me that the great John A. Macdonald has entered this hallowed hall without stumbling over himself and slurring something about railways before collapsing into his chair?

"This teetotaller across from me is not the man the people chose to lead them," he continued.

In his decade-plus career, the representative of Kingston has never before dared take his seat without consuming at least six pints the night before, plus a few sips of whisky from his flask to get going in the morning. But all that changed today, leaving even his ardent supporters struggling to defend his actions.

"Look, we all have bad days," said George-Étienne Cartier, shaking his head as he watched Macdonald effortlessly pour water into his glass without spilling a drop.

But clearly the offence was too great for some to brush aside. By noon, five Tories had crossed over to the Reform party. After Macdonald completely neglected to vomit in his desk, the governor general had no choice but to step in and demand his resignation.

"GET OFF MY RAILWAY" Tubman says before blasting slave catcher with shotgun

## Scandal! Anglican to marry Lutheran

———— JUNE 12, 1859 ————

VICTORIA, B.C. — The small, newly founded community of Victoria has been shaken to its core this morning by news that Sally Montgomery, a noted member of the Church of England, will marry Lucian Hannover, a filthy Lutheran.

"We are absolutely shocked," said Sally's Aunt Liza. "I thought dating someone from a slightly different but fundamentally quite similar Christian denomination was just a phase, a temporary walk on the wild side, but clearly I was wrong.

"This is not the Sally we raised."

Experts warn of the danger of marrying outside one's congregation, noting that the relationship will almost certainly fail since the two parties have nothing in common. Also, any children born of the marriage will be sure to exhibit significant physical and mental limitations.

But these concerns apparently mean little to the "suddenly believes in the Formula of Concord" tramp Montgomery.

"I know it's a bit controversial, but I love him so much!" gushed Sally, unaware of the pain and embarrassment she was causing her family. The Montgomerys will now be forced to eat at Lutheran restaurants and drink from Lutheran water fountains.

At press time, rumours that Jessica Northrop was courting a Jewish boy were too terrible to even be considered.

# Second Underground Railroad allows Confederate soldiers to escape to Canada

———— NOVEMBER 18, 1865 ————

KINGSTON — After decades of helping black Americans escape the barbarism and brutality of southern slavery, the United Province of Canada has created a second Underground Railroad in order to aid Confederate officers and government officials as they avoid prosecution by fleeing to Canada.

"It is our duty to help those seeking freedom, whether it be a slave who refuses to be shackled, or a former slave owner who mutinied against his country in order to keep shackling other humans," said Canadian government spokesman William Wenthrop.

"After secretly supporting the Confederacy throughout the American Civil War, this was the least we could do."

Already dozens of men have made it across the border, hidden in bourbon casks, shipments of cotton, or caskets, of which there are so many these days. Though they have only just arrived, many, such as Colonel Jackson Montclair, say they feel right at home.

"The weather is cold here, but the people are warm. I do not need to hide my presence or my service to the beloved Confederacy. The Canadians do not mind at all!"

Montclair added that, although not yet a Canadian citizen, he really appreciates that he already has more rights than every black Canadian he's met.

**WATCH OUT!**

**IS YOUR NEIGHBOUR A FENIAN?**

HERE ARE SOME CLUES:

1. His last name begins with "Mc," unless he's Thomas D'Arcy McGee—he's okay
2. Incessantly sings "Down by the Glenside" or "Avenging and Bright," and romantically plays a tin flute near a stormy coast, longing for his homeland
3. Fails to compliment your Oliver Cromwell painting
4. Will tell you how his day has been in a wonderfully eloquent, well-crafted poem
5. Attends Fenian meetings, sometimes referred to as "going to Catholic mass"

*If your neighbour demonstrates one or more of these traits, please report him to your local Orange Order lodge.*

A Public Service Announcement from
THE GOVERNMENT OF CANADA

## British North America Act

Everyone knows a few of the lines from the British North America Act, the document that gave Canada its independence. Items like the promise of Peace, Order and Good Government as well as the division of responsibilities between the provinces and federal government are widely read as early as elementary school. But how well do you know these lesser known provisions?

### BRITISH NORTH AMERICA ACT

Whereas the provinces of Canada, Nova Scotia, and New Brunswick wish to form a sovereign Dominion, it is hereby resolved as follows.

...

235. All schoolchildren outside of Quebec shall be taught enough French that they will claim to speak it when talking to other anglophones, but when someone tries to speak French with them they will immediately retract their claim and say they are "rusty."

...

303. All cities/towns in the new country will have a Queen Street and a King Street. They shall run east–west when the monarch is a woman, and be turned north–south when it is a man.

...

378. Ketchup. Ketchup on everything.

...

429. Every small town shall have a minimum of 10 and a maximum of 20 women named Barb.

...

516. You all hate the city of Toronto now. Don't question why.

...

576. The province of Quebec shall be empowered to protect the French language by acting super condescendingly to anyone speaking English.

...

610. Public infrastructure must be kept in such a state that it is always decaying, useless, or otherwise incredibly outdated.

...

638. Gravy and cheese on French fries. Just trust us.

# PATH TO CONFEDERATION

*Economics and the need for a national approach to security (especially from a hostile United States) encouraged Canada and the Maritimes to unify into one country. But would Britain simply let its colonies go, or would the desire for independence turn into a bloody revolution similar to that which had taken place in America a century earlier? Nah, turns out the Brits were super chill about it. Provided Canada could get its shit together.*

## George Brown struggles to narrow pro-Confederation speech to a three-hour sound bite

———— FEBRUARY 8, 1865 ————

QUEBEC — Clear Grit Parliamentarian George Brown was reportedly up most of last night attempting to narrow his address in support of Confederation into a succinct three-hour sound bite.

The Reform politician is expected to make his case to his peers in the Legislative Assembly on the benefits of creating a political union with the province of Canada, New Brunswick, and Nova Scotia, but has had little success narrowing the speech down to a brief 250,000 words from the original 678,000 words.

"Blast! I cannot cut my Plato reference to creating an Upper Chamber, which will represent the wisdom of the philosopher kings," decried Brown to himself who was overheard in the corridors of the assembly. "Without these references to great glories and exploits in our human history, from Cleisthenes and his noble

constitutional reforms of Athenian democracy and the magnificent Magna Carta restricting the powers of King John in 1215, to the failures of the pigheaded American constitution that lead to the Civil War, and our current predicament of political deadlock in the United Province of Canada, someone may accuse me of being boring, but on the other hand . . ."

According to servants at his homestead this morning, Brown still hadn't completed his sentence.

© 1983 Luke Huntley, Esq.

12 11 10 9 8 7 6 5 4 3 2 1                    1 2 3 4 5 6/9

First printing

# YOUR DESTINY AWAITS

It is 1864. You are Sir John A. Macdonald, leader of the Tory party and the person who's been in charge of the United Province of Canada for many years. Will you be able to bring in French Canadians and the Maritime provinces, create an independent country, and maintain this decent buzz you've got going?

You're in your office, trying to figure out how to justify using public money to build the railway line that will go from your front door right to your favourite tavern. You've had four ales and a whisky and are feeling Pretty Good, if you know what I mean. All of a sudden, in walks George Brown, leader of the Reform party, editor of *The Globe* newspaper, and a total dick. You continue working for a while, pretending not to notice him, but eventually he clears his throat loudly in that annoying way you've heard him do so many times before.

"What is it, George?" you ask (stopping yourself from adding "you motherfucker").

"We need to make a change, John," he replies. "The union of Upper and Lower Canada is failing. And as its civil war ends, America will be looking to annex us. Plus, our economy is stagnant. The only solution is for the creation of a new country, one that's united economically and militarily."

How do you respond?

You take a breath, stand up, and punch George Brown in his smug face. You then throw him and his foolish ideas out of your office. Go to page 2.

You take a long drink and stare George Brown down for a moment before finally agreeing. You promise to make it your top priority. Go to page 3.

1

You really didn't understand the point of this game, huh?

Go back to page 1 and start again.

You know the key to getting this deal done will be ensuring the support of the Lower Canadian delegation. You need to meet with your old friend George-Étienne Cartier. What do you do?

Go to his home. Go to page 4.

Meet him at a tavern. Go to page 5.

What are you thinking? You know George doesn't keep any good scotch at home. Get your head on straight, John!

Start again.

George is late, yet again, which gives you time to "do some preparation" for the meeting, in the form of three lagers and two shots of something called "Devil's Tongue." When George does arrive you get straight down to business and explain the proposal. Unfortunately, he does not appear receptive.

"Why would the people of Quebec support this? We want independence from the British, not union with British colonists!"

How do you respond?

Carefully explain to him that Confederation will allow Quebec's French Canadian population to have control over important matters like education, health care, and culture. Go to page 6.

Offer to build him his own railroad. Go to page 7.

"Not a bad answer, John, my old friend," he replies. "With that guarantee I can promise the support of the Quebec representatives, provided you do me a favour." Cartier pauses, then looks into your eyes and whispers the word "railroad."

Go to page 7.

One little railroad later and the support of French Canada is in the bag. But the work is far from over. The Atlantic provinces, which you do not know and where you have no allies, have not yet agreed. What do you do?

Go on a pub crawl through the entire Maritimes to get to know the East Coasters better. Go to page 8.

Arrange for a formal conference in Charlottetown to discuss the matter. Go to page 9.

You stumble into your tenth Argyle Street pub of the night. You haven't slept in days as you've travelled throughout New Brunswick, PEI, and the southern coast of Nova Scotia, drinking your fill at every location. Your head is pounding and you can feel the rot in your stomach. Plus, they won't. Stop. Playing. The. Fiddle. You're ready to give up and go home when you notice that seated in the corner are Charles Tupper, Samuel Leonard Tilley, and John Hamilton Grey, the premiers of Nova Scotia, New Brunswick, and PEI, respectively.

You know that this is your moment. You approach them with a bottle of scotch and join their table. After several hours of drinking and telling hilarious stories about a prostitute back in Kingston, you get down to business. What will it take for the Atlantic provinces to join the new nation of Canada?

You can tell you're winning them over. Sure, you'll have to build a few more personal railroads, but within a few minutes they will agree to the proposal. All of a sudden, a strong, sea-weathered hand grabs your shoulder from behind. You turn and see him: Newfoundland premier Hugh Hoyles.

"Come from away 'der boi? We don't want nunin ta da wit your Confederation. I suggest ya be an your wai."

Hoyles lifts you out of your chair and pins you against the wall. You have only moments before he throws you out of the pub. What do you do?

Give a detailed, passionate speech about why Confederation is a good idea—and that it will create a proud nation of Canadians who will look back on the brave men who founded the country as heroes. Go to page 10.

Attack like your ancestors taught you. Go to page 11.

The Charlottetown Conference is a smashing success! Within a few hours all attendees have agreed on a framework for how the new country will function, including the division of powers between the provinces and the federal government. All concur that you shall be sworn in as the first prime minister, cementing your place in the nation's history.

Just one problem: In all the planning you completely forgot to keep drinking, and now you're stone-cold sober. Better try again!

Start again.

Before you've even gotten to the meat of your point about manufacturing tariffs, that old sea dog Hoyles is waving you off.

"Too late for speeches, me son. Time for talk is ov'r."

He lifts you by the collar and tosses you through the doors and into the street. As you lie there, a puddle soaking through your trousers, you can hear the laughter of the other premiers. You know you've lost them, and that the dream of Canada is dead.

Head back to page 1 to see if you can do better!

Your right cross catches Hoyles by surprise, sending him reeling. But he's been in more naval brawls than you can even imagine, and within a moment he's back on his feet, charging. The fury of his attack is overpowering, but you use your advantage in reach to hold him off. For the next several minutes you wear each other down. Although you land a few solid jabs, he nearly completes the takedown.

Finally, when he's least expecting it, you unleash your secret weapon: a roundhouse kick to the temple. The Newfoundlander crashes to the floor.

You pause and then chug the remains of the scotch bottle in one go. You look over at the premiers, triumphant. They hesitate, but then let out a hearty cheer and begin applauding your victory. Finally, their people are free from the tyranny of Newfoundland. They immediately sign their names to the British North America Act you've been carrying in your pocket all along.

Congratulations! You managed to create an independent Canada and get totally drunk at the same time.

# The Beaverton.

PUBLISHED EVERY SO OFTEN } *when the mood strikes*

*"North America's Trusted Source of News—THE EDITORS."*

SATURDAY, OCTOBER 12, 1867.

{ SIX DOLLARS PER ANNUM: SINGLE NUMBERS 3C.

WHOLE NO. 1-10

## INDIANS THANKED IN SPECIAL COLONIZING CEREMONY

OTTAWA – Canadian parliamentarians and Canada's first Governor General were on hand to pay homage to the Indians who once were stewards of the land that is now Canada.

"We must express our gratitude for the natives who guided our first explorers, fought with us in wars against the Americans, and surrendered their territories so that the land may be exploited with farmland and factories," read His Excellency, The 4th Viscount Monck, to the gathering of MPs and Senators on the lawn of Parliament Hill. "As is positive Canadian custom, I would like to say thank you, as this nation could never have colonized anyone without you."

As per tradition, no Indian tribes were present during the ceremony. However, the spectacle did feature a treaty burning ceremony that legally absolves the new federal government of any promises made to the natives.

## PATERNITY TEST CONFIRMS SIR JOHN A. ACTUAL FATHER OF CONFEDERATION.

PART NOS. ¼ ½ ¾

### PM OWES BILLIONS IN CHILD-REARING RELATED COSTS.

OTTAWA – A paternity test has confirmed that Canada's first prime minister, Sir John A. Macdonald, is the actual Father of Confederation.

Queen Victoria said that Confederation was conceived by Macdonald on a hot September night in 1864 in Charlottetown. She is now demanding roughly $88 billion in child support payments.

"He's the deadbeat dad of Confederation," said a sassy Queen Victoria. "He drinks excessively, hasn't seen Confederation in years, and spends his whole time trying to build a silly railway. It's about time he gets real and starts taking care of something he helped create."

A belligerent Macdonald appeared before a booing studio audience.

*"Canada's baby daddy."*

"Confederation isn't my baby!" claimed the visibly inebriated PM. "There were 35 other guys in her life. How could Confederation be mine? I never intended on having provinces! Look at her birthmark! Bicameral legislatures? Hell no! Not my child!"

The audience erupted in shock after Macdonald revealed that the

queen was fraternizing with his longtime rival Oliver Mowat, the premier of Ontario.

"She was hanging around with that muck snipe Mowat all evening at the Quebec Conference," Macdonald clarified.

In another twist, George Brown, D'Arcy McGee, George-Etienne Cartier, and several other men have claimed to be the father of Canada.

"I promised to protect the queen from those dangerous Americans and take care of her debts," Cartier explained. "I will always remember the passionate evening when we decided to divide powers between provinces and the federal government."

Before the moment of truth, McGee and Brown engaged in a round of fisticuffs and were promptly tackled by security.

After the test confirmed what many had suspected all along, a devastated Macdonald sank back into his chair and took a long drink from his flask.

## ENGLISH CANADIANS CELEBRATE SLIGHT DIFFERENCES FROM MOTHER COUNTRY

ST JOHN – The British subjects of Canada have marked the first Dominion Day by noting their subtle differences in music, art, sport, fashion, and world perception from the people of their imperial homeland.

"Yes, we speak the same language, have the same Queen, and are dictated to by British Parliament in decisions about foreign affairs, but let's celebrate how almost half of us were born in Canada," said Fletcher Bernard Cambridge, raising a glass of whiskey to his fellow Anglo-Saxons in the pub. "And sure, we fly the same flag as Britain, pray to the same God, and enjoy a good football match, but, er, it's colder here and we're damn proud of that!"

Cambridge's impromptu address drew applause and three hip-hip-hurrahs. The rather raucous evening ended after a cricket match and the singing of the Canadian version of God Save the Queen.

# National

## PUBERTY

### (1867–1914)

"The 19th century was the century of the United States. The 20th century will belong to Canada. The 21st will be split between Australia and Thailand. And the 22nd will belong to the Galactic colony of Guatemala."   Wilfrid Laurier

Having accidentally thrown off the yoke of colonial oppression they'd desperately wanted to maintain, the Fathers of Confederation were faced with a new task: how to turn a barely connected country of French and English, Maritimer and Mainlander, Métis and Full-Blood into a united people. Their efforts would cement the Canadian identity we know today: a country constantly in search of an identity.

# KEY DATES

**June 24, 1880**
O Canada played for the first time, spontaneous hockey game breaks out

**October 10, 1885**
Strongman Louis Cyr lifts a record breaking 2,400 grocery bags

**November 3, 1887**
Election day enters tenth month

**June 6, 1891**
4 million Canadians wake up with raging hangovers from Sir John A. Macdonald's wake

**July 11, 1895**
Canadians already forget the name of the new prime minister

**July 10, 1895**
Mackenzie Bowell becomes prime minister

**October 11, 1898**
Canadians who signed up to wear funny pith helmets unaware they're being sent to fight in the Boer War

**April 4, 1899**
Dawson City bar unveils gold-plated puke bucket

**August 4, 1910**
HMCS *Rainbow* becomes Canada's first warship to honour the LGBTQ community

# Unlike Prussia or the Ottoman Empire, Canada does not have what it takes to last as a country

*By Lord Halverton*
*Winston Calverton III*

———— DECEMBER 1, 1867 ————

KINGDOM OF BAVARIA — It has been a few months since we "celebrated" the birth of a new country, and it is time we face up to some hard truths. As a British man I have travelled the globe and gotten to know many nation states inside and out. As something of an expert on the topic, I can say with certainty that, as opposed to Prussia, the nation of Canada will not survive very long.

The simple fact is that to be a country one must have a unifying ethnic and religious identity. That is what has allowed countries like England and France, and the Ottoman Empire, to be so successful, and why they will continue to dominate the global landscape until the end of time. Canada, by contrast, is torn by division of language, religion, and whether ketchup or mayonnaise is the right condiment for French fries. What chance do you have?

A nation must also be unified in purpose. Do you really think Austria-Hungary would have become the dominant, sure-to-exist-forever nation state it is if its citizens couldn't agree on a division of powers between the central government and local authorities the way Canadians can't?

But the main reason this Canadian experiment will never succeed is the country's proximity to the United States. When you have a small population and an indefensible border, it is only a matter of time before the larger entity next door swallows it up. That is why secure countries like the Kingdom of Bavaria will last forever while countries like Canada and Portugal are doomed.

---

# D'Arcy McGee's murderer to get fair trial: Judge

———— SEPTEMBER 7, 1868 ————

OTTAWA — Judge William Buell Richards says that the man responsible for killing D'Arcy McGee will get a fair and balanced trial before he's found guilty and promptly executed.

"It is my sworn duty to ensure that Mr. Patrick James Whelan will hear all the evidence illustrating that, beyond a reasonable doubt, he did kill Thomas D'Arcy McGee in the early morning of April 7, 1868," said Judge Richards while drawing a brief sketch that showed a stick figure being hanged at the gallows, the eyes on its face crossed with two "x" marks.

To ensure greater honesty and accountability of the court, Prime Minister John A. Macdonald—a close friend of the deceased—will be permitted to select the jury, coach the prosecution's witnesses, and provide financial incentives for anyone who has information or rumour that can lead to Whalen's conviction.

"Perhaps the Catholic could send in the pope for a character witness," joked Orangeman John Hillyard Cameron, who will act as Whalen's attorney. "I promise we won't have any prejudices against the Fenian bugger and will defend him until he's inevitably found at fault.

"We will also review how he pulled the trigger despite having the ill-competencies characteristic of an Irishman," he added.

In addition to the murder charge, Whalen will be tried and convicted for several other murders, thefts, assaults, and acts of witchcraft dating back to 1767.

## British Columbia Joins Confederation

*The federal government had been eyeing British Columbia—with its gold reserves and access to the Pacific—and in 1871 made a significant push to convince the province to join Confederation. While ultimately successful, these efforts came at a steep cost. Below is a list of demands B.C. legislators made, all of which were ultimately granted.*

—

## DEMANDS

A federally funded railway will be built from Ontario to the Pacific.

The federal government assumes all debt incurred by the future province.

Everyone immediately agrees that Vancouver is and always will be considered superior to Toronto.

We get to design a crazy provincial flag.

The provincial government receives 100% of the tax revenue from opium dens.

British Columbians will maintain control over the new province's suspension bridge infrastructure.

The federal government will pay for the construction of no fewer than 50 independent coffee shops every year.

# Three-way treaty between Canada, Métis, and mosquitoes creates province of Manitoba

OCTOBER 8, 1870

WINNIPEG — After years of negotiation and the suppression of the Riel rebellion, admission of the Manitoban territories into Confederation was secured yesterday evening in the form of a trilateral agreement between the federal government, the Métis, and the billions of mosquitoes that currently control the land.

"We are delighted to be able to welcome a fifth province to the Dominion of Canada," said Interior Minister Alexander Campbell. "I wish to think Mr. Riel and Buzz, the leader of the mosquito tribes, for their hard work in securing this great result.

"We have not only built a new province, but have also ensured that mosquitoes will continue to survive and thrive in that province for centuries to come."

The mosquitoes held out for months before committing to the treaty. Their negotiation tactics, which included repeatedly biting Canadian dignitaries and constantly flying by the ear of Army General Garnet Wolseley as he tried to sleep, angered many.

However, in the end they won numerous concessions, including a guarantee of tariffs to protect them from American competitors and a promise that the capital city, Winnipeg, will be built in a location that is somehow as swampy in summer as it is ungodly cold in winter.

"There is no doubt that the mosquitoes drove a hard bargain," said Campbell. "But they compromised as well, agreeing to give us one week a year after the snow melts before they descend upon the citizenry."

# Groggy PEI wakes up from bender with John A. Macdonald, discovers it has joined Confederation

JUNE 12, 1873

CHARLOTTETOWN — Nursing a brutal hangover, the entire population of Prince Edward Island woke up this morning to discover that, at some point during last night's drunken evening with Prime Minister John A. Macdonald, they had organized and voted in a province-wide election to join Confederation.

"Oh man, oh god, my head," muttered all 108,000 residents. "What happened last night . . . oh god, what did I do!

"I'm never drinking again," they added.

Although still foggy on the details, the islanders maintain that they intended to go out for only one drink with the PM as a way to mend fences after their bad breakup six years earlier when PEI rejected Confederation. But one turned to two, and pretty soon the irascible Macdonald had convinced them it would be a great idea to set up voting booths all across the island so that they could officially cast their ballot in favour of joining Canada.

---

"What happened last night . . . oh god, what did I do!" said the entire population of Prince Edward Island

---

"I think I might have been an election monitor," said Gale Ackland, shortly after chugging a large glass of water and binge-reading an entire book collection.

The referendum results show strong support for joining Canada, with 93% voting to join and only 4% electing to remain independent (3% wrote in the phrase "More whisky, please").

Residents plan to organize a province-wide brunch so that they can figure out what they'd agreed to with respect to division of powers and transfer payments. They would also like to determine whether they fell at some point during the night because their knee really hurts.

For his part, the prime minister appeared remarkably spry given that he'd spent the night drinking thousands of people under the table. He was already in the process of making plans for himself and hundreds of kegs to travel to Newfoundland.

# Newspaper notice: *The Beaverton* will deny Macdonald–railway baron bribery scandal starting at $5000

*By the Editors*

——— JULY 29, 1873 ———

OTTAWA — The editors at *The Beaverton*, North America's Most Trusted Newspaper, would like to inform Prime Minister Sir John A. Macdonald that we will not print any scandalous details about the PM's acceptance of bribes from any railway barons in exchange for the immediate delivery to our offices of $5000.

This initial offer includes our publication's overlooking this rather embarrassing and very damaging affair and instead dedicating three full pages to the St. Andrew's Church box social last week and the latest developments in the field of phrenology. Any details about the prime minister's close relationship to Canada Pacific Railway Company's Sir Hugh Allan and about bribing voters through the open ballot system in the 1872 election will be brushed aside by important classified advertisements about used book sales.

For $10,000, our publication will not only provide an outright denial but also attack the Conservative party's opponents, in particular that scoundrel George Brown and *The Globe*. We are prepared to claim that the Liberals invented this entire scandal in an elaborate partisan attempt to defame our beloved prime minister. We'll question the Liberals' patriotism and assert that if the railway isn't procured and constructed soon, an American takeover of our fair Dominion will be imminent.

For another $10,000 (totalling $20,000), we'll report that it was the Liberal opposition leader and his party who were accepting hundreds of thousands in bribes from various sources. We will also insinuate that Liberal leader Alexander Mackenzie is a pigeon-livered hornswoggler and suffers from severe incontinence.

Please leave your generous contribution in crisp $20 notes, in a letter or sack, by noon tomorrow in our mailbox at the following address:

384 Yonge St.
Toronto, ON

# Desperate Alexander Graham Bell waits all day for woman to call him back

———— AUGUST 9, 1876 ————

BRANTFORD, ON — Intrepid scientist and inventor Alexander Graham Bell has patiently waited by his newly invented electric telephone for a very critical call from a lady he was fraternizing with last night.

"I told her where the other line was located. Why hasn't she rung yet?" said Bell at his summer homestead in Brantford as he stared at the receiver. "Maybe she's sick or got into a carriage accident."

Bell became excited when he heard a muffled vibration on his communication device.

"Mabel, is that you?" Bell said into the conic-shaped sound box before realizing the other voice was that of his assistant, Thomas A. Watson.

"Dammit, Watson! Get off the line! Yes, I know this technology is miraculous, but I'm waiting for an important call!" an agitated Bell exclaimed.

At press time, an angry mob appeared at Bell's residence demanding the release of the tiny man trapped inside his invention.

# The Indian Act

*The Indian Act was passed by Parliament in 1876, making it Canada's oldest piece of legislation aside from the Constitution. Although often criticized as being "unrelentingly racist," the final draft of the Act is actually an improvement over the first draft, sections of which are reproduced below along with notes/corrections from PM/Justice Minister John A. Macdonald.*

---

*Confidential.*                                                 *Revise,* 11 *Apr.* 1867.

British North America.                                          5

## DRAFT

OF AN

~~ACT TO DESTROY~~

~~THE~~

~~SAVAGE INDIAN~~

~~WITHOUT HAVING TO~~

~~KILL HIM YOURSELF~~

FOR

**The Union of the British North American Colonies, and for the Government of the United Colony.**

WHEREAS it is expedient to amend and consolidate the laws respecting Indians : Therefore Her Majesty, by and with the advice and consent of the Senate and House of Commons of Canada, enacts as follows :          *Pre-amble.*

*Preliminary.*

**1.** This Act may be cited as The Indian Act.          *Short title.*

*Interpretation & Definitions.*

**2.** The term "Indian" means a person who ~~we demanded put themselves on a government list or else we wouldn't give them any money or land~~ is registered as an Indian or is entitled to be registered as an Indian.          *Indian.*

**3.** The term "child" ~~means a person we are going to kidnap from their homes and place into schools in a deliberate attempt to destroy their racial and religious identity, all of which was made legal by this act~~ includes a legally adopted child and a child adopted in accordance with Indian custom.          *Child.*

**4.** The term "reserve" means a ~~small portion of the land we took, which we are now forcing you to live on in order to maintain your status~~ tract of land, the legal title to which is vested in Her Majesty, that has been set apart by Her Majesty for the use and benefit of a band.          *Reserve.*

**5.** The term "intoxicant" means alcohol, the sale of which to Indians is expressly banned under penalty of six months' imprisonment, ~~because as we all know Indian people are children for whom the government must decide what they can drink, even though we have been selling/trading them alcohol for years and the high levels of alcoholism in their communities are directly our fault.~~          *Intoxicants.*

*Status.*

**6.** A person will lose their rights as a status Indian for the following reasons:          *As to rights.*
[Here would follow :
  1. *Marrying a man who is not a status Indian.*
  2. *Voting in a federal election.*
  3. *Having at the age of 21 a mother or paternal grandmother, who did not have status before marriage.*
  4. *Being born out of wedlock to a mother with status and a father without.*]

*no Changes needed — great work — Jno. Macdonald*

(0.17.)                    A                              *Union.*

# Sandford Fleming invents time-zone machine

———— OCTOBER 15, 1879 ————

TORONTO — Canadian inventor Sandford Fleming has wowed scientists and the world by inventing a "standard time-zone machine" capable of transporting man into the past by one hour or into the future by one hour or more.

When Fleming presented his invention at the Royal Canadian Institute, scientists were aghast at what will inevitably disrupt the "time-space" in both past and future by establishing time zones based on degrees of longitude. Fleming claims that his machine can transport anyone who crosses a border on a map forward or backward into time based on whether they head east or west.

The gentlemen of the Royal Canadian Institute were curious, if not baffled, by the intrepid inventor's new device and how it works.

"Mr. Fleming's contraption has the power to hasten my travel from Halifax to Montreal by one full hour," exclaimed Dr. Fred Yelmick of King's College. "Remarkable!"

Others were disturbed by the prospect of an apparatus that dictates the past and future from Ceylon to Winnipeg.

"What will man do if this time-zone travel machine is placed in the wrong hands?" questioned Queen's College professor Zachary Jedediah Smith, an expert in the study of phrenology. "This could lead to massive disruption of dates and making me late for tea time. Wars could be started or prevented. As noble men of science, we must destroy Mr. Fleming's idea at once! At once, I say!"

Although the presentation at the Royal Canadian Institute caused a great stir, scientists appear to be content with determining time based on examining the innards of a dead animal.

# The only reason I became a doctor was to look at penises

*By Dr. Emily Stowe*

———— JULY 16, 1880 ————

I didn't become one of the first physicians in our Dominion to help the sick, or even to illustrate a point about how women are just as capable, competent, and professional as men. No, I did not overcome the prejudices against my feminine sex and practise medicine just to inspire little girls so they wouldn't face the same kind of obstacles as I did. To be clear, I was solely motivated to look at as many penises as possible.

While many of you may think this is perverse, a man's jack-in-the-box is the most fascinating piece of anatomy I have ever come across. As a little girl, I once

saw the diddle on Michelangelo's *David* in a picture book and right then and there I knew I wanted to become a doctor.

The gentleman students in medical school kept covering up the genitals of the male anatomy, but I refused to be bullied over my real passion and kept redrawing phalluses over and over again. I would yell at the professor, "Less about tuberculosis and more about cocks!" and "Foreskins are our friend!" To protest my poor treatment, I replaced my signature with a quick sketch of a rock-hard gooser.

Now that I am a licensed physician, I operate my practice according to one fundamental rule: Every male patient who comes to see me, whether it be for bronchitis or a broken arm, is required to pull down their trousers and show me their flapdoodle so that I can stare at it for a few minutes before I begin treatment. In fact, I diagnose most of my patients based on the angle of the dangle.

I look forward to seeing you in my doctor's office, gentlemen!

# "AN ORAL HISTORY OF THE RIEL REBELLIONS" using the
# WILLIAM LYON MacKENZIE KING—SÉANCE METHOD.

*The rebellions of Louis Riel gave Canadian history a number of firsts. They marked the first time the new federal government exerted its military capability, the first time since Confederation that the anglophone—francophone divide became a national crisis, and the first time someone chose to live in Saskatchewan. Using a recently rediscovered séance ritual from William Lyon Mackenzie King, we were able to sit down and talk to the long-deceased participants about how things really went.*

## PART I: THE FOUR R's: RIEL, RED RIVER, REBELLION.

LOUIS RIEL [LR]: I spent my life searching for purpose. When I returned to Red River I'd been in the seminary, written poetry, and worked a number of odd jobs. But it was only when I came home that I found my true calling: pissing off white people.

JOHN A. MACDONALD [JAM]: Sure, we knew Riel and the Métis were mad about not being consulted when Hudson's Bay transferred the land to us. And yeah, appointing a white, unilingual anglophone to rule over a francophone Métis population was a bit of a risk. But I figured, fuck it, you only live once.

WILLIAM MCDOUGAL [WMD]: When John told me he was sending me into Manitoba, I thought "This is totally nuts." But that is just the kind of take-no-shit guy John is.

Even sitting here, 140 years later, I still think about how tough he was. Unfortunately, his attitude didn't do much for me when Riel and his band wouldn't let me enter the province.

PRIVATE ERIC GARNER, FORT GARRY: I was on the barricade having a smoke when I saw the Métis army approaching. I yelled to my fellow soldiers for help defending the fort, but they were all downstairs because Sgt. Hartman was teaching them the best way to kiss girls. The fort fell within minutes.

*Shortly after conquering Fort Garry, the Métis declared a provisional government with Riel as its president. In an effort to avoid further conflict, the Macdonald government agreed to negotiations; unofficially, however, a group of agitators called the Canadian Party were making their own plans.*

THOMAS SCOTT [TS]: No way was I going to live under the rule of a half-breed. As soon as Gerry fell, we assembled our men and went down there. We had a brilliant plan, but it didn't work out.

LR: It was just a few dozen men walking toward the fort through the snow. Half of them didn't even have guns . . . or gloves. They're lucky they didn't freeze to death. I would have eventually let them all go if Scott hadn't kept telling his guards he'd had sex with their mothers.

TS: Yeah, I don't know why I did that. To be honest, I'd had sex with only one of the guards' mothers, and it wasn't even that great.

LR: He didn't give me a choice. Even though I knew it meant the government was going to come after me, I had to execute him.

TS: I'll admit that as I stood there staring at the firing squad just before the end, I knew I'd made a mistake.

JAM: While that Scott mess was happening in Manitoba, we were in Ottawa hammering out a deal with representatives of the Métis provisional government. George [Étienne-Cartier] and I worked day and night and finally came up with a plan that not only appeased the Métis and allowed us to send our officials in, but also created a new province. Best of all, they didn't demand clemency for Riel for Scott's murder, so we were free to go after him.

LR: Yeah, that was fucked.

## PART II: EXILE, KINDA.

*As the government took control of Manitoba and absolutely failed to deliver on the promises made to the Métis during negotiations, Riel was forced to go into exile, where he experienced a spiritual awakening that was later revealed to be more of a mental illness.*

ADAMS GEORGE ARCHIBALD, LIEUTENANT GOVERNOR OF MANITOBA [AGA]: We totally meant to do all the things we promised the Métis, but then we realized that since we made those promises in order to get access to the territory we now had, it would just be much easier to not do them. Kind of a win-win, really.

LR: I was hanging out in the Dakota territories. I wasn't up to much, living mainly off the pension Archibald secretly gave me to stay away. But I had a lot of time to think about myself, Canada, and the Métis people. I really dug into the role we as humans play in wider society, as well as what duty we owe our fellow man to be kinder and more considerate. And I came to one pretty fundamental conclusion: I am the second coming of Jesus Christ, the lord and saviour.

JAM: The idea that Riel was in exile is ridiculous. He was always sneaking back in the country even though people wanted him dead. I mean the premier of Ontario had put a bounty on his head, for god's sake! But the voters in Manitoba kept electing him to Parliament! Thank god he never showed up. It would have been an even bigger disaster than that time I answered every question during Question Period by saying: "I'm sorry, I don't understand the question. I don't speak dumbass."

ALEXANDER MACKENZIE, NEW PRIME MINISTER OF CANADA [AM]: Every stunt he pulled——whether it was the time he popped up at a campaign rally or when he disrupted a religious service in Quebec—— they all had the same effect. French Canada loved him. English Canada wanted him shot. The divide between the two factions was irreconcilable. I haven't read the news in a while on account of having been dead for over a century, but I assume that rift has pretty much healed by now?

## PART III: THIS TIME IT'S PERSONAL, JUST LIKE LAST TIME.

*Riel would be drawn back to Canada for a final time by his Métis people. Having moved west to the Saskatchewan territories, they continued to be plagued by a government that insisted they farm rather than hunt but refused to give them adequate land to do so. In their desperation, they hoped Riel could repeat the successes he'd had at Red River. But Riel was no longer the man he once was.*

GABRIEL DUMONT, MÉTIS LEADER [GD]: We had no options. We didn't have enough food or shelter. And we were living in goddamn Saskatchewan. Living there will make people do crazy things. We'd had enough and decided it was time to fight back. And to do that, we needed a military leader. I'd fought with Louis at Red River, so I went to the United States to recruit him. It didn't take him long to respond.

LR: I am Jesus.

GD: It wasn't easy uniting the community. We had French, English, moderates, and extremists. Everyone had their own ideas on how to handle things. But we eventually managed to put out a manifesto with our grievances and requests. We weren't asking for much, really——only what we'd been promised after Red River. We knew the government would receive it in the spirit of compromise we'd intended.

JAM, RECENTLY RE-ELECTED AS PM: We took it as an act of war and immediately began reinforcing the North-West Mounted Police garrison at Battleford.

GD: When we heard that, we had no choice. We seized whatever arms we could and declared a provisional government. I personally led a band and won the battle of Duck Lake [I didn't choose the name]. We were even starting to get support from the Native tribes. And Louis was giving magnificent speeches, rallying the people to our cause. One night he gave a speech that I will never forget. I'll let him tell you what he said.

LR: I am Jesus of Winnipeg, the Holy Land. Grovel in my presence! I will lead my believers on a crusade to crush the evil forces that annex our territory. May the blood of our enemies flood the battlefields and my victory be declared across the land on golden chariots. The Lord has enshrined me with other powers so that my victory will be guaranteed. One day, I will come to judge the living and the dead.

GD: Things couldn't have been going better. We thought that, just as in Red River, we'd win a few small skirmishes and force the government to negotiate. No way could they get reinforcements out that far west, right? Admittedly we did forget that, in the fifteen years between the two rebellions, the government had built the Canadian Pacific Railway.

*The federal government poured troops into the territory and won a decisive victory over Riel at the Battle of Batoche. Riel personally surrendered after the battle and was placed on trial for treason.*

JAM: Originally the trial was going to be heard in Winnipeg, but I was worried the jury might be a little too ... what's the right term, not-white? So I literally amended a law just so I could move it to Regina, where we got a jury of six Scottish Protestants.

GD: We tried to convince Louis to plead insanity, but he just wouldn't do it. He knew it meant his death, but he wouldn't give them the satisfaction.

LR: Life, without the dignity of an intelligent being, is not worth having. Also, I am Jesus.

HUGH REID, JUROR: We had to convict Riel of treason; there was no doubt that he'd committed the crime. But given the circumstances, we recommended the death penalty not be ordered. Of course, the judge laughed us out of the room and ordered him to hang.

HONORÉ MERCIER, QUEBEC POLITICIAN: French Canadians were livid that Riel was to be hanged. So angry we stopped being racist about his ethnicity, and you know how rare that is for us. We did everything we could to stop the hanging. But we failed.

JAM: I had no qualms about hanging Riel. Although, admittedly, by that point in my life I was drunk pretty much all day every day, so I don't remember a ton to be honest.

*Riel died by hanging on November 16, 1885. The Métis rebellions of the 19th century died along with him. Unfortunately, conditions for the prairie Métis would only worsen in the coming decades. Although beloved by many, Riel remains a controversial figure in much of the 10% of English Canada that knows who he is and what the word "Métis" means.*

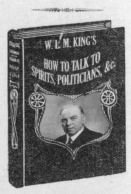

To recieve a free copy,
send $2.00 [S&H] & S.A.E c/o
THE BEAVERTON

*Driving the Golden Spike, by Hon. D. A.*

# First white man to perform manual labour on CPR drives in last spike

——— NOVEMBER 7, 1885 ———

EAGLE, B.C. — The Honourable D.A. Smith has made history in our Dominion after being the first distinguished, wealthy white man to perform any labour by driving in the last spike of the Canadian Pacific Railway, thereby uniting the province of British Columbia with the rest of Canada.

The task wasn't easy; labourers had to deliver a few blows with the maul just to get things started for the corporate leader. Then finally, after his 19th try, Mr. Smith made a direct hit, driving the iron nail into the last plank. The crowd cheered this mighty accomplishment for his race.

An out-of-breath Smith said, "My many thanks to the supervisors, who employed Chinamen for such difficult tasks as exploding nitroglycerin to break mountains, laying the tracks, and ensuring that no white man, notwithstanding the Irish, lifted a finger before I arrived to see its completion."

After photographs were taken, the distinguished banker immediately departed. Items left by dead labourers were picked up as mementoes and overdue pay.

# Macdonald balances budget after returning empties

OTTAWA — Prime Minister Sir John A. Macdonald has balanced the nation's treasury this year by taking all his scotch, wine, and beer bottles back to a liquor merchant in exchange for the tremendous sum of $27,038,948.16, putting the nation's finances back into the black.

Boxes after boxes were carted out of Earnscliffe yesterday afternoon by the prime minister and his finance minister, the Honourable Archibald McLelan, who was responsible for keeping an accurate count of the empties. After 19 years, the bottles took up most of the PM's house, including three bedrooms, the study, and any free space on every desk. It took the pair four hours to recover all the Molson Brewing containers from the garage and shed.

"The prime minister has been saving up this investment for several years," said a perspiring McLelan whilst carrying the boxes out of Macdonald's buggy. "The number of empty bottles in the reading room alone will pay for the interest on the CPR, plus the ammunition used by the militia, and if I have accounted correctly, all MP

## Single cow holds up nation's railway

salaries for the next five years."

Macdonald was happy to receive a two-cent return on each empty he gave to the merchants. The country's new surplus was, however, immediately spent on a keg of Sleeman's.

## Lazy eight-year-old still has no job

AUGUST 4, 1886

MONTREAL — Despite being a full 96 months old, local resident Simone Gervais has completely failed to find a job at any of the local factories.

"I don't understand—he's got all the qualifications necessary," said mom Marie. "A first-grade education, tiny hands and fingers for getting into the gears of machines when they break down, and a complete lack of protection from child labour laws. But he just won't get off his ass.

"I thought his father and I had raised him better than this."

With the Industrial Revolution

finally taking off in Canada, factories and sweatshops are in need of cheap, adorable labour to help produce the nation's commodities. But Gervais appears to be more interested in lounging around the house and going to school than joining the workforce.

"I've offered him a ton of positions—mechanic, munitions tester, guy who crawls into the turbine of an engine while it's still going—but he just isn't interested," said local businessman Husky Heathright.

Heathright added that although he was sick of chasing Gervais, he may be willing to give him one last shot the next time a child's death opens up a position at his factory.

When reached for comment, Gervais appeared unrepentant about his carefree, loafer lifestyle.

"I just want to enjoy a little bit more time as a child before I enter the workforce. Also, I think my tin whistle band has a real chance of making it."

## Anti-Invasion Propaganda

*Even after the Canadian provinces united in a collective defence against invasion, the threat of an American attempt to annex Canada remained quite serious throughout the latter half of the 19th century. To discourage American aggression, the federal government placed anti-Canada propaganda in American newspapers.*

—

## UGH CANADA!

Have you guys heard how terrible Canada is? I heard the snows come all year long. Wouldn't want to invade during a snowstorm! And their people are strange. The English ones are so boring and the French ones are so . . . French. It must be difficult for anyone, let alone a conquering foreign power, to try to rule over them.

Plus, they all have a terrible odour, and making love is illegal there except on Tuesday mornings. Oh, and they hate beer. All of it. And wine. Canadians drink only peach schnapps and that gross kind of whisky with cinnamon in it.

Also, Canada lacks any kind of valuable natural resources.

Anyway, just wanted to write to let you know how happy you should be that you don't have to go there!

# *Peach-basket vandal invents new sport*

——— DECEMBER 28, 1891 ———

SPRINGFIELD, MA — A man suspected of destroying dozens of peach baskets by cutting holes in the bottom has invented a new indoor game.

"Basket ball" involves five players on each team, a ball, and the senseless, deliberate destruction of perfectly good wooden fruit containers.

"It was a cold winter and we had to keep the lads active in the gymnasium," said Ontario-born James Naismith, the mischief-maker who caused several cents' worth of property damage. "I also wanted to avoid the roughhousing of most other sports. So, I positioned two [now utterly useless] peach baskets on either side and each team had to score points by getting a soccer ball into a basket."

Naismith ruthlessly sawed out the bottoms of the basket so that no one would have to climb up on a ladder to fetch the ball. This despite having numerous other items, such as barrel hoops, that need not require such savagery inflicted upon them.

Meanwhile, New England peach farmers announced that, owing to the dearth of usable baskets, there will be no harvest this year.

# Canada experiences immigration boom after ship gets lost on way to U.S.

——— AUGUST 23, 1892 ———

TORONTO — The nation's immigration rate reached a new high yesterday after a ship of Irish immigrants got lost on the way to New York and docked in Toronto by mistake.

"Is this America, the land of the free?" asked one adorable Irish child, still waving the Stars and Stripes flag she'd brought with her on the month-long journey.

"Um . . . yup," replied the immigration officer.

Canadian officials, in desperate need of immigrants to work the many factory jobs created by the Industrial Revolution, attempted to hasten the new arrivals into processing, sidestepping their questions about where the Statue of Liberty was and why New York City had so many streets and buildings named after the British royal family.

"We figure if we keep them here long enough to stamp their passports and allow their ship to leave, by the time they figure it out they'll just give up and stay," said officer Mark Hewlett.

Officials tried distracting the Irish with "Name the American President" games, but it wasn't long before some began to catch on. Surprisingly, most were okay with their altered destination.

"We're just happy to live in a country free of sectarian violence and rampant poverty," said P.J. O'Brien. "Plus, as immigrants, it's nice to feel wanted."

# The NWMP Wants You!

Aided by the Gold Rush, Canada's population began to expand north and west into communities such as Dawson City, Yukon. Filled with prospectors, saloons, and brothels, these towns are thought of as lawless—as representing the last vestige of Wild West–style behaviour. In reality, a force called the North-West Mounted Police, precursor to today's RCMP, kept a firm grip on the situation, preventing people from getting too rowdy. Here's an 1889 Help Wanted ad for the NWMP.

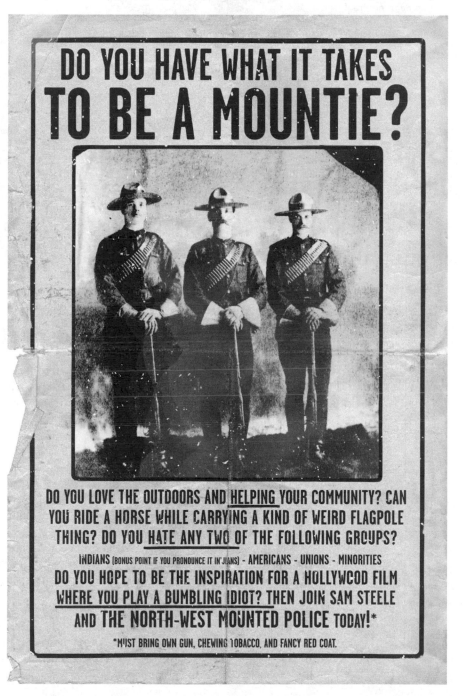

## Today's Railway Catastrophes

—

Grand Trunk pile-up near Montreal

Head-on collision between freight cars, passenger train in Brandon

Incomplete railway bridge collapses outside Quebec City

# Quiet whisper of "gold" causes human avalanche of prospectors

———— JULY 6, 1896 ————

DAWSON CITY — An estimated 200 people are dead in a Klondike crush involving thousands of prospectors after someone gently whispered the word "gold."

The terrifying phenomenon occurred when a local resident made an observation to himself about the possibility of gold in Rabbit Creek, Yukon Territory. Frightened locals began to witness a tremendous swarm of bodies rolling down the surrounding mountains.

Trees and river beds were knocked aside in the sudden rush of mostly American miners, who nonetheless appeared to be digging up everything in its wake.

"That's my flake of gold and you ain't getting it!" yelled one prospector to the giant pile of men surging above and below him, all armed with shovels, pans, and pickaxes.

"You're on my claim, you son of bitch!" yelled another ambitious prospector as he tumbled downward—his last words before he was swept away in a sea of humanity.

Recovery efforts are underway, but rescue teams are being delayed by poor conditions and their own insatiable desire for gold.

# *Canada's Gymnastic Formation Team gives Boers a drubbing with human pyramid assault*

FEBRUARY 27, 1900

PAARDEBERG, SOUTH AFRICA — The 14th Royal Canadian Gymnastic Formation Team has given the Boers a real licking at Paardeberg by deploying a formidable human pyramid.

The successful attack occurred in the early hours, just after the Canadians had completed their daily calisthenics and before proudly donning their Maple Leaf–patterned unitards.

"We used a low-cover human-fan lineup to approach the front line without being detected," said Captain H.L.F. McInnis, MC. "Then, when the firing began, we took decisive action by assembling into a tight, instantaneous stand-up pyramid while four men covered the left flank with a human windmill formation to act as a decoy."

The Canadians came just in time to relieve the 7th Australian Vertical Rope Climb Brigade, who'd suffered significant casualties under heavy fire and were thus unable to reach the top of the rope.

Intense combat ensued, but the team managed to get in range to set off a medicine-ball barrage, showering the enemy with three 15-lb. weights.

The cowardly Boers promptly fled the battlefield after witnessing the Fighting 14th's demonstration of teamwork, gymnastic prowess, and aerobic conditioning. The feisty flying Canucks had won the day, and the battle, for the British Empire.

# Marconi's First Trans-Atlantic Spam Messages—1901

*In December 1901, Guglielmo Marconi transmitted the first trans-Atlantic spam message from Cornwall, England, to Cape Spear, Newfoundland, in order to appease the sponsors of his wireless experiments.*

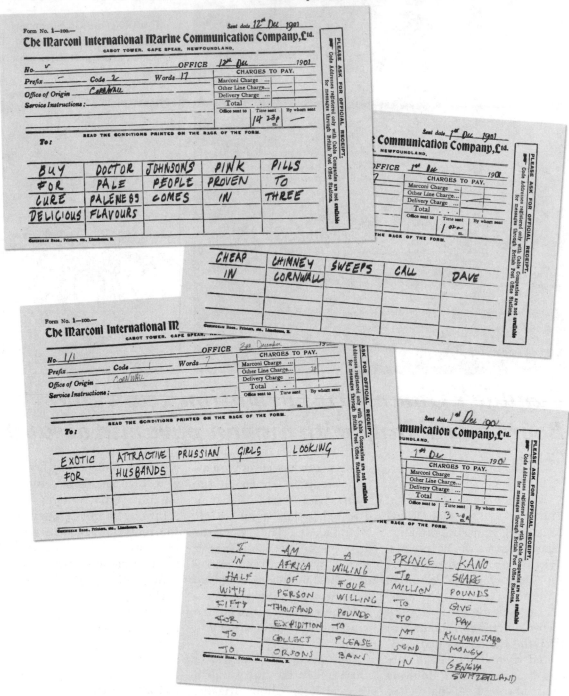

Form No. 1—100.—

## The Marconi International Marine Communication Company, Ltd.

CABOT TOWER, CAPE SPEAR, NEWFOUNDLAND.

Sent date 12th Dec 1901

No. ✓    OFFICE 12th Dec    1901
Prefix —    Code 2    Words 17
Office of Origin    CORNWALL
Service Instructions :

CHARGES TO PAY.
Marconi Charge ...
Other Line Charge...
Delivery Charge ...
Total
Office sent to    Time sent    By whom sent
14 23p

PLEASE ASK FOR OFFICIAL RECEIPT.
Code Addresses registered only with Cable Companies are not available for messages through British Post Office Stations.

READ THE CONDITIONS PRINTED ON THE BACK OF THE FORM.

To:

| BUY | DOCTOR | JOHNSONS | PINK | PILLS |
| FOR | PALE | PEOPLE | PROVEN | TO |
| CURE | PALENESS | COMES | IN | THREE |
| DELICIOUS | FLAVOURS | | | |

Cushingham Bros., Printers, etc., Limehouse, E.

---

Sent date 1st Dec 1901

Communication Company, Ltd.
NEWFOUNDLAND.

OFFICE 1st Dec    1901

CHARGES TO PAY.
Marconi Charge
Other Line Charge
Delivery Charge
Total
Office sent to    Time sent    By whom sent
1 02 m.

PLEASE ASK FOR OFFICIAL RECEIPT.
Code Addresses registered only with Cable Companies are not available for messages through British Post Office Stations.

THE BACK OF THE FORM.

| CHEAP | CHIMNEY | SWEEPS | CALL | DAVE |
| IN | CORNWALL | | | |

Cushingham Bros., Printers, etc., Limehouse, E.

---

Form No. 1—100.—

## The Marconi International M

CABOT TOWER, CAPE SPEAR, N

OFFICE 2nd December    19

No. 1/1    Code 1    Words 7
Prefix    
Office of Origin    CORNWALL
Service Instructions :

CHARGES TO PAY.
Marconi Charge...
Other Line Charge... 28
Delivery Charge...
Total
Office sent to    Time sent    By whom sent
m.

ASK FOR OFFICIAL RECEIPT.
Code Addresses registered only with Cable Companies are not available for messages through British Post Office Stations.

READ THE CONDITIONS PRINTED ON THE BACK OF THE FORM.

To:

| EXOTIC | ATTRACTIVE | PRUSSIAN | GIRLS | LOOKING |
| FOR | HUSBANDS | | | |

Cushingham Bros., Printers, etc., Limehouse, E.

---

Sent date 1st Dec 190

munication Company, Ltd.
OUNDLAND.

1st Dec    190

CHARGES TO PAY.
Marconi Charge ...
Other Line Charge...
Delivery Charge ...
Total
Office sent to    Time sent    By whom sent
3 20 m.

PLEASE ASK FOR OFFICIAL RECEIPT.
Code Addresses registered only with Cable Companies are not available for messages through British Post Office Stations.

THE BACK OF THE FORM.

| I | AM | A | PRINCE | KANO |
| IN | AFRICA | WILLING | TO | SHARE |
| HALF | OF | FOUR | MILLION | POUNDS |
| WITH | PERSON | WILLING | TO | GIVE |
| FIFTY | THOUSAND | POUNDS | TO | PAY |
| FOR | EXPIDITION | TO | MY | KILIMANJARO |
| TO | COLLECT | PLEASE | SEND | MONEY |
| TO | ORSONS | BANS | IN | GENEVA |
| | | | | SWITZERLAND |

Cushingham Bros., Printers, etc., Limehouse, E.

# Riding barrel over Niagara Falls now leading cause of death in Canada

*Laurier demands Canadians cease senseless Falls stunts unless they're double-dared*

———— OCTOBER 23, 1901 ————

NIAGARA FALLS — Physicians in Ottawa have determined that Canada's leading cause of death is riding over Niagara Falls in a barrel.

"More than 10,000 souls have perished while hurling themselves over the Falls this year alone," explained Dr. John Ross Blithe. "We should be discouraging these acts, whether they're born of curiosity, a desire for racing, a compulsion for betting, or any other tomfoolery. Why people have such a drive for these reckless stunts is beyond me."

Dr. Blithe paused for a moment, presumably to reflect on the mighty roar of the Niagara, one of Mother Nature's greatest waterfalls.

"But to speak frankly, I'd really like to see someone finally do it."

Some have lost their entire family to what could have been glory, popularity, and a very entertaining ride that one day could turn into a successful tourist business.

"I lost two brothers, my father, mother, and grandmother to the Plunge," lamented a young Cheryl Smyth. "My Uncle Dave thought he could survive by riding in a barrel made out of solid lead. When he put it in the river, it sank so quickly that he didn't have time to escape. He didn't even make it over the Falls. That's why I'm trying an iron barrel instead when it's my turn tomorrow."

Niagara barrel plunging beat out the other leading cause of mortality in the country: riding in high-speed carousels.

# Race rioter mortified after using Chinese slur on Japanese immigrant

——— SEPTEMBER 9, 1907 ———

VANCOUVER — Niles Hawkins, a white Vancouver man who's been participating in the days-long riot against Orientals' being allowed to immigrate to British Columbia, was chagrined yesterday to learn that he'd mistakenly used a Chinese-specific slur on a Japanese man.

"I was breaking the windows of an apartment in Chinatown when I saw him. I guess because of the location I just assumed he was Chinese.

After the man advised him of his true ethnicity, Hawkins immediately apologized and frantically attempted to correct the situation, to no avail.

"I tried my hardest to let him know that I realize not all Asian people are the same. I asked him if he liked sushi, I even mentioned geisha girls. But I could tell he just thought I was racist."

Eventually Hawkins was forced to give up and, under a cloud of guilt and shame, resume destroying businesses and attacking people at random.

For his part, the man he'd encountered, Riku Watanabe, admitted to being offended by Hawkins's actions.

"I'm sure he isn't a bad guy, but that kind of cultural insensitivity is really harmful, especially in this day and age. Now, if you'll excuse me, I have to go hide."

# Anne of Green Gables starts bar fight

——— JUNE 21, 1908 ———

AVONLEA, PEI — A disgruntled orphan, Anne Shirley of Green Gables, began another bar fight at an Avonlea pub, sending a number of men to the town's doctor.

Witnesses from the scene at Rooster's pub explained that the fight began after a local bully antagonized the red-headed girl by calling her "Carrots" while she was trying to enjoy her scotch. In response to such torment, the ragamuffin broke a beer bottle over the head of one Gilbert Blythe.

Several rounds of fisticuffs ensued, but Anne Shirley gave all her opponents a real licking, landing every punch on the jaw, nose, stomach, and groin.

"What's wrong with that girl?" asked Mr. Phillips, a schoolteacher who'd had his nose broken and a tooth knocked out during the donnybrook. "She's ruined my date with one of her pupils. She will receive a most severe scolding tomorrow in class!"

Despite the best efforts of the burliest of village men, no one could restrain the child.

"She felled Reverend Allan!" exclaimed Mr. Barry, pointing at Avonlea's holy man, who was lying unconscious among the broken glass and spattered blood. He had attempted to reason with the mad girl as she was tossing bar stools and tables out the tavern's windows.

Marilla Cuthbert, Anne's adopted mother, says there must have been a mix-up at the orphanage, and that she plans to return the destructive child tomorrow in exchange for a calm brown-haired girl.

## The Original Top Gun: Silver Dart

*After its first flight in 1909, the Silver Dart inspired a romantic-uction-drama film about a daring aviator who gets the opportunity of a lifetime when he's selected to fly in the elite Wright Brothers' School for Really Slow Aircraft in North Carolina.*

J.A.D. McCURDY — ALEXANDER GRAHAM BELL — KELLY McGILLIS

# Silver Dart

"IT'S TIME WE BUZZED THE TREES!"

"I FEEL THE NEED. THE NEED TO PRODUCE LIFT IN MY AEROPLANE."

SPEEDS OF UP TO A ROARING 40 M.P.H.!
TERRIFYING 25-FOOT ALTITUDE! ONE MAN, ONE MACHINE!

# Emily Carr asks Haida to move totem poles into better lighting

———— MAY 10, 1912 ————

CUMSHEWA, QUEEN CHARLOTTE ISLANDS — Famous Canadian painter Emily Carr has asked the Haida elders of Cumshewa on Moresby Island to move their ancient totem poles a little to the left in order to get better lighting.

The towering, centuries-old cedar totem poles were slightly dappled with the shadow of a few tall spruce trees. Although the framing was excellent, the composition was not quite right. Carr could see immediately that a new and better arrangement was required to create the desired effect.

"The culture of the Pacific Northwest people has been such an inspiration to me," said Carr as she made a rough sketch of where she wished the poles to be repositioned. "But, unfortunately, the lines—the light—it doesn't properly capture the beauty that I and modern Canadian society are looking for. I've asked the elders to move them. I think they'll get on it right away."

The 41-year-old artist, known for her eccentric life and her foray into a male modernist style, has made it her mission to preserve the culture of the Haida people. She firmly believes that this is best achieved by representing their ancient works in an artistic genre that Vancouver art critics favour and understand. Sometimes, as in this case, that means shifting around ancient relics.

Importantly, Carr also avoids presenting living subjects in her paintings, as that would disturb the immensely popular assumption that the Indians are all dead.

*The first Calgary Stampede, in July 1912, was a real hoot for everyone involved, except the horses.*

## *A Women's Parliament:* Worst burlesque show ever

### *Show hard on political messages, soft on nudity*

*By Beaverton theatre critic Kenneth Walters.*

——— JANUARY 29, 1914 ———

WINNIPEG — For those of you thinking this "mock Parliament" would be a good time, don't bother. The posters for the show indicated songs and girls. Sounded like a blast, so my buddies and I decided we'd check it out.

When a group of ladies came out on stage in black cloaks, we got pretty excited, thinking they were going to do a sexy dance or something.

We were promised a controversial performance. But instead of revealing any tassels or feather boas, they just stood around in those cloaks talking like a bunch of men. I know women talk a lot, but can't they do it while bathing naked in a giant champagne glass?

At one point, some pretty young thing took centre stage. Just when it looked like she was going to show us a little skin, she launched into an impersonation of the premier. Definite boner kill.

What is so funny about a bunch of women acting like men? I don't get it.

# Denial of Entry into Canada: SS *KOMAGATA MARU*

——— JULY 23, 1914 ———

*According to immigration officials at the time, passengers on the SS* Komagata Maru *were definitely not denied entry into Canada because of racism.*

Denial of Entry into Canada: SS *Komagata Maru*

Sir,

We are writing to inform you that your ship and its passengers must leave Vancouver immediately. The reason for your denial is that we have found many violations with the vessel. They are as follows:

The deck was a little wet.

A few scratches were on the bow and a nickel-sized dent was in the back.

The ship is surrounded by water.

The ship made a stop in Hong Kong rather than a non-stop voyage from India.

The ship makes a rocking motion with the waves.

We can assure you that these and these alone are the absolute only reasons we will not let you enter or disembark. Leave the harbour immediately or you will be fired upon.

Have a pleasant day!

H.H. Stevens
Malcolm R.J. Reid

## TOP 10 WORDS
## to drink to at your next temperance meeting— pocket card game

Temperance meetings can be a real buzzkill on a Saturday night. The next time someone takes you along to straighten you out, or to "see some friends," make sure to have this list of words (and your flask) in your pocket!

SNEAK A SHOT EVERY TIME SOMEONE IN THE MEETING SAYS OR DOES THE FOLLOWING:

...

1. Sin
2. Devil
3. Stands up
4. Sighs loudly
5. Prohibition
6. The lord
7. Teetotal
8. Jesus
9. Drunk
10. Spirit

# The Beaverton

No. 34521       12 PAGES       TUESDAY, AUGUST 4, 1914       Edition anglaise       ONE PENNY

# NATION READIES ITS ONLY GUN AS WAR IS DECLARED

Prime Minister Borden introduces the "Wingham Rifle" to the troops!

## CANADA'S ROSS RIFLE EXPLAINED

The place where, presumably, the bullets come out?

Patented Ready–to–Jam™ bolt mechanism

Gunsight with miniature poster of Lord Kitchener saying "I want you to aim"

Cartridge that contains at least 50% bullets

Chinese finger trap trigger

Edible butt

OTTAWA—The Borden government is calling on the country to mobilize its only functioning rifle after war has been declared on Germany and her allies. The safely stored weapon, which has not been fired since the Boer War, was found in a Wingham, Ontario home.

"This ought to show the Hun we mean business," declared Prime Minister Borden while blowing off the dust on the Lee-Enfield first produced in 1895. "Along with our cricket wickets and hockey sticks, this will make us a formidable army." Canada's only line of armed defence came with twelve rounds of ammunition, a cleaning rod and a half-full bottle of whiskey. Borden cautioned his troops that guns are quite dangerous and whoever handing the

gun should be at least 21 years of age and have proper safety training.

Already there was fierce competition amongst our boys as to who would get to actually carry the rifle into battle. Eventually it was decided that the honour ought to belong to Cpl. Nathaniel Haywright, who had the highest proficiency score at the army's BB Gun competition. After Haywright fires a shot he will hand over the rifle to the soldier with the next highest score.

### ALOOF MILITIA MINISTER SAM HUGHES IMMEDIATELY SENDS TROOPS TO MICRONESIA

Not wasting any time after the declaration, Minister of the Militia Sam Hughes

immediately deployed 25,000 soldiers to distant Pacific islands to defend against the German presence in Nauru. Citing the strategic importance of the islands coconuts and sand supplies feeding the Kaiser's army in Europe, Hughes ordered his hastily trained men to storm the exotic tourist destination. Equipped with his swimming trousers and straw hat, Hughes personally strolled through the captured territory and seized the colony's beach chairs and umbrellas and declared the sundrenched location to become Canada's new Pacific Headquarters. Hughes' victory is the first in what many expect to be a glorious, warm conflict.

*(See "Gun" on p. 12)*

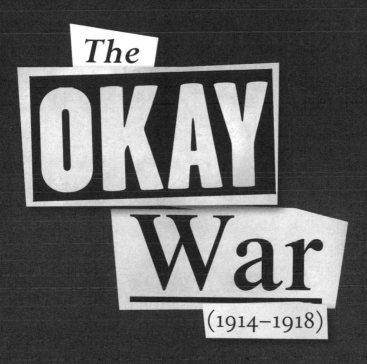

# The OKAY War

## (1914–1918)

"I am terrified. A blinding flash and an explosive howl a few feet in front of the trench. Acrid smoke bites the throat. I am beyond mere fright. I am frozen with an insane fear. This war shall end me. But I know it shall be worth it in order to preserve the borders of Serbia, France, and Belgium." – Unknown Canadian soldier

A national history would not be complete without explosions, marching, and killing people while singing campfire songs. In 1914, Canada fought her traditional enemy. No, not the Americans or the Métis or the Irish; it was the Germans this time. Heroes flocked to the flag, gaining glory and the honour of having dozens of obscure geographical landmarks named after them. On the homefront, Suffragettes like Nellie McClung were transforming Canada by helping women win the right to vote even though they only wanted everyone to stop drinking booze. It was the war to end all wars except for all the ones that followed.

# KEY DATES

**June 28, 1914**
Serbian man unwittingly sets
off European powder keg while
trying to get light for cigarette

**November 12, 1915**
Heroic messenger pigeon Bert earns
Canada its first Avian Cross

**July 1, 1916**
Germans overwhelmed by dead bodies
being hurled at them at the Somme

**April 9, 1917**
Canadian soldiers enjoy view from ridge

**September 20, 1917**
Billy Bishop scores his 72nd mistress

**March 15, 1918**
Community dying of influenza clearly
not doing its part for war effort

**November 11, 1918**
War ends when Robert Borden beats the
Kaiser in a jitterbug dance competition

**September 1, 1919**
Small town thankful for new
memorial park, grateful for veterans'
sacrifice so that it could be built

# Canadian military recruitment strategy expands to reach new audiences with "The war that will be over by Chanukah" campaign

——— SEPTEMBER 9, 1914 ———

OTTAWA — The federal government today launched a new recruitment drive aimed at encouraging ethnic minorities to join the battle against the Boche.

Since the outbreak of war in August, military recruiters have been mounting a furious campaign to increase enrolment numbers. They're now hoping to draw on the support of Jewish Canadians, along with such other groups as Asian Canadians and First Nations, with targeted promotions.

"We encourage our most loyal and patriotic Jewish citizens to join in the good fight," said government communications director George Baldwin. "We've almost got the Hun licked. Sign on to bear arms in Europe and you'll be back to light the menorah in no time!"

The campaign asserts that once more Canadians join the fray, German morale will collapse sooner than the eight nights the candle stayed lit for the Maccabees. It goes on to claim that German soldiers will be "flattened like latkes!"

> "We've almost got the Hun licked. Sign on to bear arms in Europe and you'll be back to light the menorah in no time!" said communications director George Baldwin

Planned follow-ups include "The war that will definitely be over by Chinese New Year's" and "The war that'll wrap up by summer solstice at the latest!"

## IN THE NEWS

1914 Berlin, Ontario, Oktoberfest has been cancelled: No refunds

Sophisticated French troops prefer to choke on Dijon mustard gas

Militia Minister Sam Hughes leads charge against own troops on donkey

Allied tanks terrorize Germans by falling in ditch, catching on fire

**EIGHT WAYS TO KNOW WHETHER YOUR NEIGHBOUR IS ACTUALLY**

# THE HUN!

1. Puffball on toque is actually a spike
2. Has a picture of the kaiser instead of the kaiser's grandmother, Queen Victoria
3. Spells names and places with a "k" instead of a "c"
4. Puts mustard gas on everything
5. Flies a Zeppelin to work instead of a Sopwith Camel
6. Lacks a Union Jack tattoo on either forearm
7. Wantonly bayonets innocent women and children (just like in the posters!)
8. Does not give all his pay and property to Canada War Bonds

*Sponsored by*
CANADA WAR BONDS

# MAZE: Find your way out of the trenches

*Learn just how fun the Great War is by completing this maze. These labyrinths are located all over continental Europe, so take a French vacation from the comfort of your home. Fight the Hun the way the Tommies do and see if you too can get out alive!*

## Innovative captains of industry discover cheaper, more efficient labour method called "employing women"

———— MARCH 30, 1915 ————

MONTREAL — While our brave boys are off fighting Fritz on the front line, industrialists have adopted a new cost-saving production method: hiring those of the feminine persuasion.

While many expressed concern about dainty hands contaminating deadly munitions with care and compassion, innovative business leaders note that female employees are willing to be paid less for the same amount of work. These patriotic dames, who earn less than half of what their male counterparts do, are also posing for such inspiring posters as "We Can Do It—for Half Price!" and "My Other Blouse Is a War Bond."

"We call this innovation the 'wage gap,'" explained general manager Joseph Flavelle of the William Davies Packing Company. "We've seen it work in the teaching and medical professions, so we decided to take a risk and try it out on the factory floor. And what results!"

"It's my privilege to help my country," said new employee Lindsay Gwyer. "Not my right, just like voting."

While the women seemed just as at home making bombs as they were at making biscuits, the program backers did wish to assure an uneasy public that, when the war ended, these women would return to their domestic virtue.

## Women's childbearing hips too wide to fit in voting booth, say men

———— JANUARY 31, 1916 ————

WINNIPEG — Despite desperate pleas regarding hip span from gentlemen in the field of lady studies, the Manitoba government is going ahead with plans to give the vote to all women.

"Voting booths are too narrow for the shape of a woman," explained Alistair Matthews, leader of the recently founded Protection of Voting Booths, an all-male organization. "That scoundrel Agnes Macphail wants to destroy our longstanding voting traditions and make wide-hipped women feel claustrophobic. This evil must be stopped!"

However, Premier Tobias Norris steadfastly refused to listen to male experts on the destructive consequences of granting female suffrage. The legislature unanimously passed a bill permitting women to cast a ballot in the next provincial election.

Science has demonstrated that a woman's posterior acetabular rim can be five degrees wider than a man's, far exceeding the width of a typical voting station, says Matthews, who admitted he hadn't calculated whether the women could avoid bruising their hips by turning to the side.

At press time, men were warning about the dangers of hysterical women voting during their time of the month.

# Military censorship being ███ to ███ war's progress

███ of the war.

With Canadians participating at ███ and ███, nerves were ███ and the battle went ███. Losses were tremendously ███ with many men ███ and even more ███. Generals were ███ and sending their men to a certain ███.

███
███
███
███
███

———— AUGUST 12, 19██ ————

███, ON — The freedom of the ███ is at stake with ███ ███ being censored on the ███.

███
███
███
███
███ toast. Germans were ███ defeated. Prisoners were ███, ███, and ███ before they met a shallow ███. Irking the ███ was the discovery that their ███ had already been ███ before any of the ███ men had opened them.

Prime Minister Robert ███ said he would look into ███ ███, but sources say there are ██ ███ men to continue the fight.

# Billy Bishop shoots down entire German air force

———— JUNE 2, 1917 ————

ARRAS, FRANCE — Canadian fighter ace Captain Billy Bishop of the Royal Flying Corps has shot down the entire German Imperial Air Force, capping his aerial victory count at 3268.

When awarded the Victoria Cross for an earlier solo mission in which he bagged seven aircraft at an enemy aerodrome, Bishop stated that he'd single-handedly put German air power out of action for the rest of the war.

"I lined up five enemy machines in my sights and blasted them with a single shot," a stalwart Bishop told his fellow pilots while illustrating his dog-fighting manoeuvres with his hands. "'Take that, Kaiser!' I yelled after making my 1529th kill. He never saw me coming."

After running out of ammunition, the cunning and resourceful Bishop used any object he could find in the cockpit to throw at Fritz.

"The Red Baron went down after a direct hit with my left shoe," Bishop noted.

Bishop went on to say that after concluding his mission, he immediately bedded all the downed pilots' widows.

# Winnie the Pooh's enlistment records

*The black bear that inspired A.A. Milne's Winnie the Pooh was a veteran of the Great War. As the regimental mascot for the Fort Garry Horse, Pooh fought in France and Flanders and was wounded twice. He received a Military Medal for charging and mauling a German machine gun team.*

## Description of ..... Winford Turkienicz ..... on Enlistment.

Apparent Age ..... 2 years 9 ..... months.
(To be determined according to the instructions given in the Regulations for Army Medical Service.)

Distinctive marks, and marks indicating congenital peculiarities or previous disease.

(Should the Medical Officer be of opinion that the recruit has served before, he will, unless the man acknowledges to any previous service, attach a slip to that effect, for the information of the Approving Officer.)

Is a bear.

Height ..... 6 ft. 8 ins.

Chest measurement { Girth when fully expanded ..... 48 ins.
Range of expansion ..... 6 ins.

Complexion ..... Bushy.

Eyes ..... Black.

Hair ..... Everywhere.

Religious denominations {
Church of England .....
Presbyterian .....
Methodist .....
Baptist or Congregationalist .....
Roman Catholic .....
Jewish .....
Other denominations ..... Church of the
(Denomination to be stated) Latter-Day Saints

### CERTIFICATE OF MEDICAL

I have examined the above-named Recruit and find ..... of rejection specified in the Regulations for Army Medical Se.....

He can see at the required distance with either eye ..... free use of his joints and limbs, and he declares that he is n.....

I consider him* ..... Fit ..... for the Canadian .....

Date ..... November 9th ..... 1914

Place ..... St. Gabriel-de-Valcartier, Que.

*Insert here "fit" or "unfit."

Note.—Should the Medical Officer consider the Recruit unfit, he will fill ..... been attested, and will briefly state below the cause of unfitness:—

### CERTIFICATE OF OFFICER C.....

..... Winford Turkienicz .....

inspected by me this day, and his Name, Age, Date of Attes ..... been recorded, I certify that I am satisfied with the correctn.....

Date ..... NOV 9 1914 ..... 191 .

---

### ATTESTATION PAPER ORIGINAL Nº 11882

Folio.

#### CANADIAN OVER-SEAS EXPEDITIONARY FORCE.

##### QUESTIONS TO BE PUT BEFORE ATTESTATION.
(ANSWERS)

1. What is your surname? ..... Turkienicz.
1a. What are your Christian names? ..... Winford "Winnie".
1b. What is your present address? ..... White River, Ont.
2. In what Town, Township or Parish, and in what Country were you born? ..... Forest, Canada.
3. What is the name of your next-of-kin? ..... Orphaned by hunter.
4. What is the address of your next-of-kin? ..... Another forest, Canada.
4a. What is the relationship of your next-of-kin? .....
5. What is the date of your birth? ..... Two winters ago.
6. What is your Trade or Calling? ..... Being a bear.
7. Are you married? ..... Single and looking.
8. Are you willing to be vaccinated or re-vaccinated and inoculated? ..... Yes, especially for rabies.
9. Do you now belong to the Active Militia? ..... Yes—Fort Garry Horse.
10. Have you ever served in any Military Force? ..... No.
If so, state particulars of former Service.
11. Do you understand the nature and terms of your engagement? ..... Yes.
12. Are you willing to be attested to serve in the CANADIAN OVER-SEAS EXPEDITIONARY FORCE? ..... Yes.

##### DECLARATION TO BE MADE BY MAN ON ATTESTATION.

I, ..... Winford Turkienicz ..... do solemnly declare that the above are answers made by me to the above questions and that they are true, and that I am willing to fulfil the engagements by me now made, and I hereby engage and agree to serve ..... dian Over-Seas Expeditionary Force, and to be attached to any arm of the service ..... of ..... or during the war now existing between Great Britain and Germany sho ..... ear, and for six months after the termination of that war provided His M ..... services, or until legally discharged.

Date ..... Nov. 9th ..... 1914.

..... (....ure of Recruit)
..... (....ature of Witness)

##### OATH TO BE TAKEN ..... .....TION.

I, ..... Winford Turkienicz ..... that I will be faithful and bear true Allegiance to His Majesty King Geo ..... Successors, and that I will as in duty bound honestly and faithfully defend H ..... ccessors, in Person, Crown and Dignity, against all enemies, and will observe and ..... esty, His Heirs and Successors, and of all the Generals and Officers set over me. So he.....

..... (Signature of Recruit)

Date ..... Nov. 9th ..... 1914. ..... John Bird ..... (Signature of Witness)

##### CERTIFICATE OF MAGISTRATE.

The Recruit above-named was cautioned by me that if he made any false answer to any of the above questions he would be liable to be punished as provided in the Army Act.

The above questions were then read to the Recruit in my presence.

I have taken care that he understands each question, and that his answer to each question has been duly entered as replied to, and the said Recruit has made and signed the declaration and taken the oath

before me, at ..... St. Gabriel-de-Valcartier, Que. ..... this ..... 9th ..... day of ..... November ..... 191 4

..... (Signature of Justice)

M.F.W. 23
750M—3-15
R.Q. 1772-89-341

# "In Flanders Fields": First Draft, 1915

*John McCrae's powerful poem romanticized the sacrifice of soldiers during war, but required a few versions and edits. Here is the first draft. An edited version later appeared in* Punch *magazine*

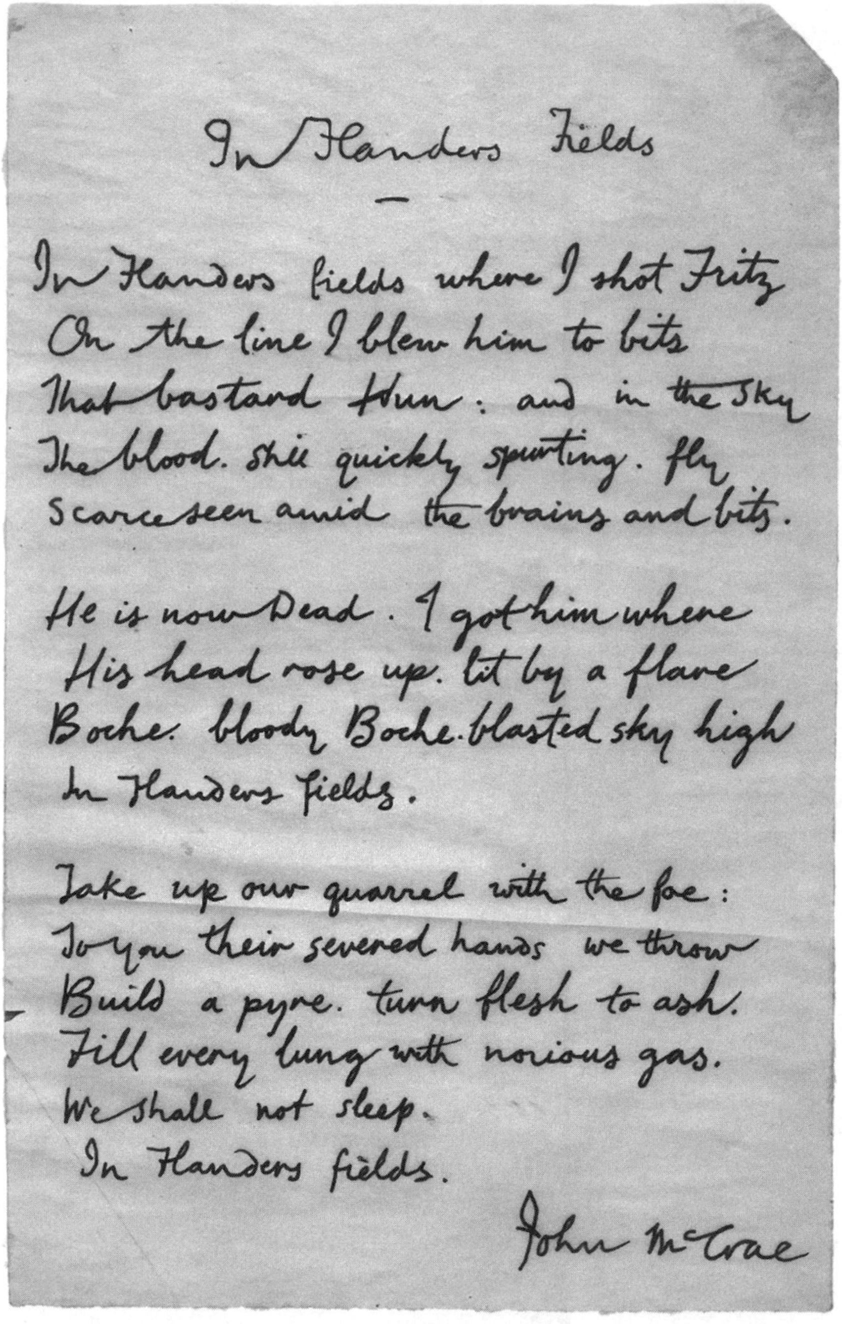

In Flanders Fields

—

In Flanders fields where I shot Fritz
On the line I blew him to bits
That bastard Hun: and in the sky
The blood. still quickly spurting. fly
Scarce seen amid the brains and bits.

He is now Dead. I got him where
His head rose up. lit by a flare
Boche. bloody Boche. blasted sky high
In Flanders fields.

Take up our quarrel with the foe:
To you their severed hands we throw
Build a pyre. turn flesh to ash.
Fill every lung with noxious gas.
We shall not sleep.
In Flanders fields.

John McCrae

## 1916 Summer Olympics to feature 100-metre "No Man's Land Dash"

—————— AUGUST 11, 1916 ——————

BERLIN — Officials today released more details on the upcoming Summer Olympic Games. The Olympic Committee of Berlin, selected to host the 1916 games over Ypres and Gallipoli, has announced that the premiere event will be a 100-metre dash through a desolate killing zone located between two trenches.

"Compared to those in ancient Greece, today's athletes demonstrate their abilities in new and different ways, and we feel that our modern Olympics should reflect that," said Jacques Cliquot, vice-president of the International Olympic Committee. "There is no better test of a man's athletic prowess, physical stamina, and mental fortitude than asking him to run at an enemy line, screaming and with bayonet pointed, through a devastated landscape filled with the body parts of animals and people."

Critics have pointed out that both spectator and participant numbers are expected to be lower than previous years, owing to the ongoing violent conflict raging across much of Europe. Many national organizing committees are considering conscription should volunteer athlete numbers prove inadequate.

Officials remain confident that the games will encourage international understanding and peace through sporting competition.

Other events to be introduced at this year's Olympics include trench pole vaulting and synchronized shell-crater diving.

## Beloved Halifax brothel spared in explosion

—————— DECEMBER 7, 1917 ——————

HALIFAX — In a miraculous story of survival, Halifax's most beloved brothel, Miss Harrington's Cathouse, remained virtually untouched by a massive explosion that killed thousands and levelled the city.

"Oh, thank god! I mean, what is that?" said the city's mayor.

Maids at the bawdy house were reportedly shaken but uninjured by the gigantic blast. They'd been shielded by the building's sturdy brick structure, as were the dozens of soldiers and sailors inside, along with some of the city's most notable pro skirts.

Other men, trapped in rubble around the city, made sure to inquire about the prostitutes' safety.

"Is Clarissa okay?" said one man pinned under the bricks and mortar that were once his home. "And Cybil? And Mary? Please tell me they made it out alive.

"And please don't tell my wife."

—

AMONG THE LOSSES
OF THE EXPLOSION:

—

250 tons of TNT
2,367 tons of picric acid
62 tons of gun cotton
246 tons of benzol

GONE, BUT NOT FORGOTTEN

# British hail Canadian troops for their unique ability to steal other people's lands

FEBRUARY 13, 1917

PARIS — The British General Staff are praising Canadian troops once more for their ability to seize land that's never been their own—a longstanding Canadian tradition.

"The young Dominion has a tremendous amount of experience gaining large swaths of territory that traditionally belonged to other people," said Field Marshal Douglas Haig. "These Canadians have wit, determination, and the ability to force the enemy onto small reserves of land with little or no negotiation. I'm very impressed with these colonial shock troops."

Noting Canada's previous military campaigns against the Iroquois, the Cree-Assiniboine, the Métis, and every other Native group, the commander of the British Expeditionary Force explained that Canadians have a unique capacity to hang on to inhospitable land where they're not welcome.

"And the Canadians hold their ground despite vicious counterattacks. They dig in permanently by establishing fortifications, farms, and curling rinks. They're now calling one-fifth of Belgium 'New Canada' and refusing to cede any gains to anyone, including the Belgians. Magnificent!"

The compliment from British High Command was well received among the men, who were busy capturing land at Ypres (now referred to as "New Calgary") and knocking down the ruins of a medieval church and cemetery in order to establish an 18-hole golf course and clubhouse.

# Jingo Bingo

*Jingo Bingo was a popular game with Canadians during both World Wars. Many found it to be a fun, exciting way to pass the time and make people feel different.*

# British Generals Award Selves Victoria Crosses

*Victoria Cross medals were the British Empire's highest distinction for bravery. But in the world's first global conflict, for which millions laid down their lives, there were more stories of sheer heroism than anyone could keep track of. How did the generals decide who the honour should go to? Fortunately, they were able to simplify matters by giving it to themselves.*

—

## LIST OF VICTORIA CROSS WINNERS FOR 1917

**FIELD MARSHAL SIR DOUGLAS HAIG** — Field Marshal Haig has demonstrated courage by gallantly ordering Canadian and British soldiers to bravely die in the mud of Passchendaele. Haig endured a barrage of objections and contrary advice, but steadfastly refused to comply with any logic. For Haig's outstanding ability to sacrifice everyone under his command, King George V will grant him this highest honour.

**LIEUTENANT GENERAL HENRY SEYMOUR RAWLINSON** — Deep behind friendly lines, Lieutenant General Rawlinson captured a good hors d'oeuvres table at the Allied Officers' Ball on October 28. Despite repeated advances by the French and American General Staff, Rawlinson aggressively repelled the hungry belligerents from seizing any of the canapés and caviar from the tray by throwing his body in front of it and using his high-society small-talk training as a clever distraction. Rawlinson managed to hold his position for a full 10 minutes before Field Marshal Haig and the other British General Staff could reinforce the position and exploit the tasty finger foods.

**MAJOR GENERAL WILLIAM MARCUS TUNNEY** — Lacking the soldier-servant whom he'd nobly sent to the front lines as reinforcement, Major General Tunney did gallantly and heroically serve himself tea on the afternoon of October 17. Tunney went beyond the call of duty by standing up, pouring water into a kettle, and operating a gas stove. After realizing that his kitchen was low on tea, Tunney dashed across several salons in the General Staff Headquarters, retrieved a fresh batch, and returned to the stove before the water boiled. Tunney was slightly wounded after being splashed by hot water on his left pinky, but managed to carry on despite his injury and ensure that his tea was served at 4:00 p.m. local time.

# Fierce battle rages in Belgium over correct pronunciation of "Ypres"

———— APRIL 23, 1915 ————

BELGIUM — Our brave Canadian troops found themselves in the midst of some of the fiercest fighting in the war to date after they and German soldiers in the opposite trench disagreed on how to pronounce the name of the closest town.

"If we get through this, I'm going to have a nice cup of tea back in Wipers!" shouted Corporal George Bartlett, who had just shot a German soldier in the face.

"Uh, it's pronounced *Ee-pers*," yelled the Huns across No Man's Land as they unleashed massive artillery shells at the Canadian line.

The subsequent skirmish over differing pronunciations saw thousands of soldiers fall from bullets, shells, and claims of cultural insensitivity. The bloodshed was momentarily interrupted by Private John McKay when his suggestion that "maybe it's *I-press*" was quickly rejected.

Finally, Corporal Bartlett shouted, "Cover me, I'm going to consult the phonetic dictionary!" before making a brave dash to his kit bag. Upon conferring with the document, Bartlett confirmed that the correct pronunciation was *Eeeps*.

At that point the bombs stopped falling and the soldiers were able to enjoy a moment's peace, until someone asked about the correct spelling of "Passchendaele."

# Vimy Ridge: Canada becomes a nation after killing Germans for Britain on French soil

———— APRIL 12, 1917 ————

VIMY, FRANCE — Following more than a century of struggle for independence and international respect, the nation of Canada was born today after several hours' fighting Germans as a colony of Great Britain on French land just 4000 kilometres from home.

"Some thought we were already a nation because of the carefully crafted legal document the Fathers of Confederation created to define this country," said historian L.P. Album, "but now we know that the key to our identity was driving a bayonet into a German soldier's skull in order to secure a ridge of debatable significance.

"I'm sure it won't even matter if the Germans take back the ridge in a few months, rendering our achievement completely moot," Album added.

The key to this shocking development appears to be Canada's willingness to joyfully celebrate a battle that cost our country the lives of thousands of young men. Australia and New Zealand, for example, have yet to develop their own unique identities because they spend all their time commemorating the sacrifices they made in Gallipoli, despite the fact that it was a complete catastrophe. Who loses to the Ottomans anymore?

The only remaining question is how such a magnificent battle was won. Military tacticians are already exalting the brilliance of Arthur Currie's strategy of not marching into our own artillery barrage this time.

# Allied victory assured after Sam Hughes joins Germans

AUGUST 22, 1918

BERLIN — Former militia minister Sam Hughes has been appointed to Germany's Supreme Army Command and already his incompetence, jealousy, and hubris have caused widespread disruption within the Hun's armies.

"On day one he insisted that all the soldiers use this Ross rifle thing, even though it jammed right away," said Field Marshal Paul Von Hindenburg. "Then, when we told him that wasn't a good idea, he ran away crying and threatened to quit until we gave in."

It's been less than a month since Hughes, wandering along the Allied front lines demanding his job back, was captured by the Germans, who believed he could be useful to their cause. Hughes was made Colonel General and given the command of 250,000 men. Under his personal direction, half of these troops became casualties within 10 minutes, the victims of a poorly executed artillery manoeuvre.

Making matters worse for the enemy, Hughes appointed his son to an ill-defined role within the German High Command that he presumably made up without consulting anyone.

After a disastrous opening campaign, Hughes requested he be promptly awarded an Iron Cross for outstanding courage that only he witnessed.

Allied generals anticipate that it will be only a matter of weeks before Fritz's war machine is completely annihilated by gross mismanagement.

# Amputees delay victory parade

NOVEMBER 12, 1918

MONTREAL — A celebratory victory parade marking the signing of the Armistice was delayed due to the sheer number of amputees attempting to make their way down Sherbrooke Street.

Marching bands, community floats on horse-drawn carriages, and people throwing confetti were idle as dozens of men leading the march—some wearing uniforms—struggled to gain forward motion with their crutches or wheelchairs, or wobbling on their stumps.

"When are we going to start celebrating our glorious victory over the Kaiser?" asked one woman holding a YWCA banner. "If we don't get to city hall by 6:00 p.m., we'll miss the bells that will toll for our brave soldiers who defended the Empire."

Thoughtful revellers began honking car horns and gently nudging the large group of invalids to quicken the pace of the mile-long parade.

Unfortunately, the procession was further delayed when a number of shell shocked soldiers mistook a car backfiring for an artillery blast. They subsequently fell into an annoying bit of hysteria that really gummed up traffic.

"North America's Trusted Source of News"

# THE beav-erton

2 cents

for newstands

morning edition

VOL / 7153

36 pgs

ISSUED ON THIS DAY....

THURSDAY

15

JANUARY

1920

TORONTO

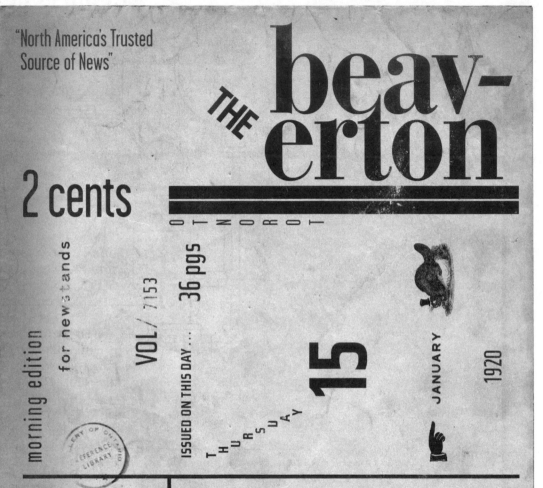

## Canadian diplomats excited to participate in high—school simulation of foreign diplomacy

## Geneva

**The Dominion of Canada** has become a founding member of the Model League of Nations, a new international body responsible for conducting world peace simulations.

Diplomats from several countries, with the exception of the United States, will try to hypothetically resolve such actual world problems as war, child labour, slavery, drug trafficking, and arms races.

"I'm looking forward to this intellectual exercise that won't have any real impact on the world," said one Canadian diplomat. "It's good to think about how this kind of international governing body would work, should one ever be created."

The teachers moderating the General Assembly, Mr. Keller and Mrs. Bianchi, were pleased to see delegates speaking about the importance of world peace, but noted that some diplomats had failed to study the League's purposes and procedures.

"This has been a learning experience for everyone," explained Mrs. Bianchi. "We think it's wonderful that these boys are talking about their nations' respective positions, but the Italian delegate keeps referring to Abyssinia as being part of his country, and I don't think the Japanese and Chinese diplomats really hit it off."

At press time, the Belgian delegates couldn't stop speaking in closed caucus in a vain effort to win the Best Delegate award.

# INTERMISSION

## (1919–1939)

"I am happy to announce that the federal government will provide a means-tested Old Age Security pension for those who have managed to live more than ten years beyond their life expectancy. Congratulations on not being dead." —William Lyon Mackenzie King, 1927

With the war over, the nation returned to its chipper, industrious ways of making various trinkets and bric-a-brac. This unprecedented time of growth and immigration was known as the Roaring 20s, followed by an unprecedented decline and amount of crying known as the Drop-Dead 30s, later renamed the Great Depression. The diets of Canadians rapidly changed from steak and cognac to leather boot tongues and fermented crabapples. Having gone from riches to rags, people waited for the good old times to return. The economy was in desperate need of a jumpstart. Fortunately, another war that needed a massive killing industry was right around the corner.

# KEY DATES

**July 10, 1920**
Arthur Meighen becomes the
first and only Canadian prime
minister who's also a lawyer

**May 27, 1922**
Canadian Club, a common cleaning
detergent in Canada, now the
bestselling bootleg liquor in the U.S.

**October 28, 1929**
Jolly good times had by all

**October 29, 1929**
Awfully rotten times endured by all

**December 11, 1931**
With signing of Statute of
Westminster, Canada finally becomes
an independent country, again

**April 10, 1933**
Dominion of Newfoundland sold for
$11.95 in British colony fire sale

**1938**
Giant tumbleweed continues to
maraud through Saskatchewan

# Winnipeg strikers demand casual Fridays

—— MAY 15, 1919 ——

WINNIPEG — Thousands of striking workers have paralyzed Manitoba's capital demanding that employees be granted the right to wear casual clothes every Friday.

Building and metal workers wearing polo shirts and hooded sweaters were the first to walk off the job, followed by sneaker-wearing telephone operators. Crowds dressed in ball caps and knee skirts began to form at Portage Avenue and Main Street holding signs that proclaimed "My Friday, My Fashion" and "Sweater Vests or Death."

"It's our right to wear more comfortable clothing on Fridays," said rail yard switchman Jacob Stilstuich in a plaid jacket. "If I want to wear a tropical-themed flannel shirt on this day, I have every right to. Long live the worker wearing an unbuttoned dress shirt!"

A.J. Andrews, leader of the Anti-Dress-Down League, stated that everything must be done to stop the savagery of such common non-work clothes as baggy knickerbockers.

"These jeans-wearing communist bohunks threaten to overthrow the common civility of the 144-hour work week!" a feisty Andrews told a crowd of wealthy industrialists. "It starts with Casual Fridays, but then they'll demand even more, such as not working on Christmas Day or refusing to die on the job."

Factory owners and businessmen claimed it was fashion interests from the runways of Paris and Rome that were coordinating the strike, an accusation denied by strike leaders.

"This is a Canadian problem," charged one of the leaders. "We will not be dictated to while the elites prosper. They grow richer while we endure endless grey trousers and suffocate in tight, oppressive bow ties."

After an altercation, the Royal Northwest Mounted Police charged the picketers, leaving two dead and a scattered pile of concert T-shirts and fancy hats littering the streets.

Mad scientist Dr. Banting discovers insulin

King–Byng fling a wingding

Federal government loses entire budget on game of blackjack

Newspapers to be printed on recycled stocks and bonds

Millionaire PM to save country from Depression, R.B. Bennett winning election motto: "I'm rich, why aren't you?"

Bindle-carrying hobo arrested for being a communist

Orwell and Hemingway join Spanish Civil War writers' retreat

# I hate my life

*By Ernest Hemingway*
*for* The Beaverton

*(Editor's note:* **The Toronto Daily Star** *refused to publish it)*

———— NOVEMBER 4, 1920 ————

TORONTO — Doctors say that death by freezing is a pleasant death. The icy winds numb you. The snows envelop you like a muffling blanket. It produces a sort of anaesthesia.

But this same death would be intolerable when set on the fringes of civilization: Melville. The dead of a Saskatchewan winter. An insufferable wasteland stretching out before you. Friendly "folk," on their way to jeer on their Million Dollar Hockey Club, stopping to impart unwanted advice and dull observations.

A man might sooner die of boredom.

I blame Mr. Hindmarsh, the lustrous editor of my soon-to-be former employer, *The Toronto Daily Star*, which he has made not fit to wipe his own fistulated asshole. I had often noted the traits of this achingly dull city filled with odious inhabitants who nonetheless travel well on skates. I made the mistake of suggesting to this editor that I would like a new role as foreign correspondent.

"You want to be a foreign correspondent?" he asked.

"To the best of my abilities," I said.

"Let's send him to Melville," said Hindmarsh.

Taking the train to Melville. Leaving a Chicago knockoff and venturing into the desolate wastes by uneasy rail.

I find myself here walking along icy, unpaved roads in the belly of this whale of a newly formed province.

I had at least hoped to meet the naked valour of man amid the stark grain elevators. Naked, no. Sooner die from cold. And valour? If I can find a farmer who will stand still long enough for a punch in the face, I will report back on the question.

This town's greatest achievement is the very railway station that called it into existence. Its namesake never made it past the 67th degree longitude, having perished on the *Titanic*, lucky bastard.

The only suggestion of a boxing ring is the town hall, where big fish in this small pond duke it out for control over naming the signposts on the main grid.

By God, I need a drink.

# Canada must end its dependence on foreign coal

*By Bernard K. Smith Jr.*

———— JUNE 5, 1922 ————

MOUNTAIN PARK, AB — Every morning I look out over a horizon laden with grey-black soot and smoke—a demonstration of a healthy, productive Canadian economy producing our household wares, our sturdy, reliable suspenders, and other key items.

But after coughing up the black phlegm in my lungs, I can't help but reflect that this coal dust wasn't mined in our fair Dominion. Rather, our power plants, factories, houses, and windmills are powered by foreign coal that comes from the shady sheiks of Virginia and Pennsylvania.

These Americans are taking jobs from workers here in Canada, workers who are more than capable of mining out the precious black rock from our own ground. Consider that the sulphur, tar, and ash that coat our homes and businesses are not of the proud Canadian variety. Our loyal chimney sweepers are inflicted with eye infections caused not by Nova Scotian black gold but by low-quality Appalachian rocks mined by some slack-jawed Kentuckian.

However, in the West there is hope and opportunity. Alberta remains one of the few places not yet touched by man's industrious hands. These peat bogs, emerald rivers, and majestic lakes contain some of the richest deposits of our country's most precious resources, and yet lie idle.

We should be seeing red that the federal government refuses to subsidize the Alberta coal fields and the necessary rail transportation to fulfill our mining and distribution needs. Five out of five Alberta coal businessmen I've talked with at my tennis club agree that the government must give more to this budding industry.

## Mackenzie King's dead mother becomes governor general

*King assures nation she gives great advice from beyond the grave*

———— AUGUST 7, 1926 ————

OTTAWA — King George V, under the advice of Prime Minister Mackenzie King, has appointed King's deceased mother, Isabel Grace King, as the 13th governor general of the Dominion of Canada.

King's mom, who can communicate to Prime Minister King only through séance, will represent His Majesty as the head of state in Canada. Her photo will now hang in every government building as a spiritual reminder of how they must all be good boys like William.

"I am very pleased that my mother has accepted this position," said the prime minister. "She provides great advice from beyond the grave. And when I told her spirit of the appointment she got so excited I thought the Ouija board was going to shatter.

"That gave a real fright to Wilfrid Laurier, my dog, and a prostitute I used to visit, whose spirits were also present," he added.

The woman who has been dead for nine years did not comment from her gravestone, but Prime Minister King says he would be pleased to take journalists back to Stornoway, where her spirit was baking cookies that he regrets not fully appreciating when she was still alive.

## Hardy Boys: The Mystery of the Disembowelled Nun

*Many Canadians don't realize that most of the Hardy Boy novels they grew up reading were written by one Leslie McFarlane, who used the pseudonym Franklin W. Dixon. McFarlane's lighthearted romps delighted young mystery lovers. Occasionally, though, his writing was criticized for being a bit too macabre. One of McFarlane's racier tales in the Stratemeyer Syndicate's series involved the lovable charges investigating the mystery of a murdered nun. Here's an excerpt.*

THE MYSTERY OF THE DISEMBOWELLED NUN      36

Another warm summer day was drawing to a close as Chip and Biff continued their game of hoop and stick in the churchyard, looking forward to their dessert of vanilla ice cream once all their chores were done.

Suddenly, a woman's scream ripped through the air.

Chip and Biff dropped their batons and bounced duty bound into action, knowing they were needed. Bravely they headed toward the location of the unexpected exhortation.

Throwing open the church doors, being sure to wipe their feet at the entrance and make the sign of the cross, they entered the nave and gasped. There at the base of the pulpit lay Sister Agatha, dead.

"It's Sister Agatha!" a stunned Chip said to Biff, who was staring at the corpse.

"Don't touch the body yet; there may still be some clues we could find," said Biff, who began to survey the blood and bowels that now covered the cathedral's granite floor. In the middle of the pool of blood Biff discovered a ritualistic dagger with the letters "L.M." carved on the handle.

"Who has the name 'L.M.'?" asked Chip, holding the sharp blade.

# Heavy Canadian accent ruins Mary Pickford's debut in talkies

JANUARY 25, 1929

HOLLYWOOD — America's Sweetheart and legendary silent film actress Mary Pickford has experienced a major setback in her first sound movie after being unable to shake her thick Canuck accent and use of un-American terms.

Early reports from United Artists studio indicate that director Sam Taylor has been frustrated with the Canadian-born actress while filming the historical drama *Cleopatra*.

Workers on the set listened as Taylor yelled at Pickford to drop her Canadian English for American English. Eavesdropping set designers heard "Mary, your character, the Egyptian Queen Cleopatra, does not end her sentences with 'eh'! It's nowhere in the damned script!" and then the sound of a megaphone being thrown to the floor.

Pickford has also constantly referred to Marc Anthony as a "keener," called the goblet of wine a "two-four," and nicknamed Augustus Caesar "bud."

The girl with the curls has never encountered a challenge like this before. In silent films, her accent was edited in the subtitles to make her sound more like a Yankee, with the letter "u" removed from such words as "honor" and "color" and "Prime Minister" written as "President."

"I'm soar-ey! I'm still learning all the American words, from A to Zed," said the actress, revealing her long-held secret.

Studio executives clarified to the press that the film will be on hold until Pickford completes her American elocution training and starts calling a sofa a "couch" rather than a "god-damned chesterfield."

# Bimbos, babes, and broads are people too

OCTOBER 18, 1929

LONDON — In a landmark decision that will surely have ramifications for years to come, the Judicial Committee of the Privy Council has extended the legal definition of "persons" to include not only "bimbos" and "babes," but also "broads."

The petition was originally brought forward by the ragtag group of bluestockings headed by the Famous Five: Henrietta Muir Edwards, Nellie McClung, Louise McKinney, Emily Murphy, and Irene Parlby. The Canadian Supreme Court scoffed at the proposition, naming it for what it was: "a bunch of applesauce from a gaggle of spinsters."

But then the British Law Lords stepped in and ratified changes to the British North America Act. It will certainly take some getting used to, but under the law the following groups are "persons" and therefore able to serve in the Senate:

Babes
Bimbos
Birds
Broads
Dames
Dolls
Flappers
Gams
Giggly wigglers
Gold diggers
Hoofers
Janes
Swanky tomatoes

The case (which had legs that went on for miles) turned on the basic principle that women are as capable as men of accepting and condoning excessive patronage, and therefore equally susceptible to all forms of corruption.

---

# One-cent gain after billions lost a clear indication of stock market recovery, say hysterical investors

*Citizens adopt fetal position*

OCTOBER 30, 1929

TORONTO — Frenzied bankers and investors have reassured the public that the one-cent gain in Western Canadian Wheat stocks at 3:12 p.m. yesterday indicates a certain economic recovery after billions were lost due to "erratic markets."

"Don't worry folks, we have this under control!" exclaimed one investor who'd just sold his pants for 50 cents in order to invest it all in the stock that he hopes will lead the recovery. "If there's any time to invest, it's right now!

"Buy! Buy! Buy!" he added before sobbing uncontrollably on the Toronto Stock Market trading floor.

Captains of industry and other wealthy men of importance say that the recovery could be aided if more regular folk would invest even greater sums in this tiny penny stock, not just their life savings.

"We need citizens to sell everything and put it in Western Canadian Wheat so that they can make some quick extra cash," noted Harold J. Morgan, who says the market recovery will make hundreds of millionaires.

At press time, the booming stock was nearing the value of several inches of tickertape.

## Bennett offers new program for unemployed: Prison

*New relief work camps offer unemployed chance to serve time*

*Thousands of impoverished men sign up for free meals, isolation*

———— OCTOBER 14, 1932 ————

OTTAWA — The governing Conservatives have passed the Unemployment and Farm Relief Act, offering the nation's jobless men an opportunity to enter prison camps and learn new skills in forced labour.

Thousands of impoverished men have signed up for the free meals and isolation. "I'm so thankful that Mr. Bennett has given me this opportunity," said one of the first voluntary inmates. "Now I won't have to get caught robbing a bank in order to get three squares a day."

The camps, to be located throughout the country's most exotic and far-flung regions, will provide vagrants with some of the best plywood bunkhouses. Among other important tasks, they'll gain experience in rock breaking, ditch digging, and wood cutting as they construct roads and bridges—critical infrastructure for the booming metropolises expected to follow.

"Some think that 30 cents a day for this type of work is too generous," said Prime Minister Bennett. "I thought so too, so that's why the government will pay them only 20 cents."

## Shack Weekly

Shack Weekly, *a popular magazine that ran from 1930 to 1936, was printed on recycled rags.*

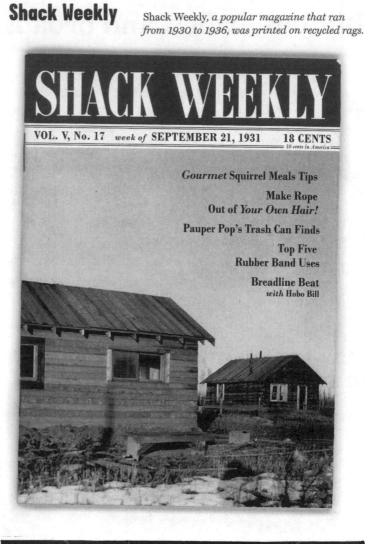

SHACK WEEKLY

VOL. V, No. 17    *week of* SEPTEMBER 21, 1931    18 CENTS
10 cents in America

*Gourmet* Squirrel Meals Tips

Make Rope Out of *Your Own Hair!*

Pauper Pop's Trash Can Finds

Top Five Rubber Band Uses

Breadline Beat *with Hobo Bill*

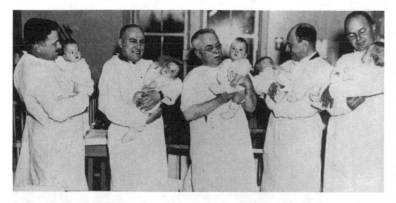

# Dionne Quintuplets remind nation that things could be worse

———— MAY 29, 1934 ————

CORBEIL, ON — The mother who managed to give birth to quintuplets has caused Canadians to reflect that their poverty would be even more devastating if they had to feed five hungry mouths.

"Please, for the love of God," said Elzire Dionne, who somehow pushed out five babies without dying, to a curious crowd gathering outside their farmhouse. "Fourteen pounds of children are just too much.

Stop staring at these freaks of nature and help us!"

Neighbours had already started forming makeshift expressions of sympathy on the Dionne family's doorstep while others dared to look inside to witness the travesty for themselves.

"What a nightmare," remarked Corrine Johnson of Corbeil, mother of twins. "How does this family ever sleep or sustain the will to live? I don't even have enough drawers in my home to make another crib."

"It's a sobering thought, which makes me appreciate my sawdust breakfast a little bit more," said Barney William Hoppner, an unemployed machinist. "Even if there were older children to help, they couldn't work for at least a few years. And thanks to misguided child protection laws, they can't be sold to a wealthy businessman like back in the old days."

Visitors from across Ontario came to see the cursed Northern Ontario family and offer their condolences for a birth more fitting of cats or opossums than humans. Others marvelled at their own circumstances by comparison.

"I have seven children and my husband left me in a tiny shack near the Don River," said a shabby-looking Martha McPherson. "I can barely clothe myself, and last week we had to eat one of my nine-year-old's leather boots. But I can't imagine having to care for five infants who can't even hold their own heads up . . . and they all survived! How terrible!"

# Indian impersonator Grey Owl has land seized, moved to reserve

SEPTEMBER 5, 1935

BEAVER LODGE, SK—Archibald Belaney, the revered Indian impersonator known as Grey Owl, has been pushed off his land to make way for lumber and mining development. Yesterday he was sent to an Indian reserve.

"We saw his demonstration on the ancient mysticism of First Peoples," said Indian agent Daniel Haberschmitt. "And we just could not believe that we were letting an Indian own private property."

The naturalist who represented "the beaver people" was finally granted his wish and treated like a real Indian. Officials at the Department of Indian Affairs will make sure that his children are taken away to residential schools and that if he tries to vote in an election he'll be disqualified.

"Since he belongs to a long-lost tribe that has no formal agreement, Grey Owl will now be living with the Cree of northern Manitoba," said Haberschmitt. "We're sure they'll welcome him as one of their own. He can teach many of the Indians on that reserve how to be better Indians with the rituals and traditional knowledge he has."

Agents also promptly shot Grey Owl's pet beaver, Jelly Roll, as beavers are considered pests who dam local waterways and obstruct hydro-electric development.

# Eaton's Unveils Its 1936 Line of Barrels

*Eaton's department stores, the country's largest, offered Canadians the most up-to-date fashions for the era.*

# Canada leads world in fastest antiquated ship technology

—————— JUNE 12, 1938 ——————

LUNENBURG, N.S. — The speediest schooner in the North Atlantic, the *Bluenose*, has once again demonstrated the Dominion's superiority in outdated technology that has no practical purpose other than racing.

Skipper Angus Walters and his crew have taken this year's International Fishermen's Trophy, beating the Yankee competitor, the *Gertrude L. Thebaud*, by three minutes—a feat that could have been accomplished much faster with an engine.

"She's an old lass, but she performed as good as ever," said Captain Walters, who's apparently never heard that ships have been powered by steam for over a century.

After a distinguished career in which it's won several International Fishermen's Trophies by re-enacting a now virtually useless trade, the *Bluenose* is expected to retire as a shipwreck.

# Nation in peril: King one day behind on latest journal entry

*Canadians lost, despondent without dull observations made by PM*

—————— DECEMBER 15, 1938 ——————

OTTAWA — Early reports from Parliament Hill indicated that Prime Minister Mackenzie King hadn't yet made yesterday's entry in his diary, causing many to variously speculate that King is severely ill, has been kidnapped by communist sympathizers, or is suffering from a broken typewriter.

The news broke early, after a Stornoway housekeeper discovered that King had failed to write any inconsequential remarks about his activities for more than 24 hours.

Citizens took to the streets, concerned that the latest tedious, outright boring details of King's life as prime minister may be lost altogether. What historians will say about yesterday, December 14, in the Lord's year of 1938, when King did not record a single observation about the daily routine of government—from what time he woke up to votes in Cabinet on the Wheat Board—is a mystery.

"How will I tell my children about the void in our history regarding what Mr. King had for breakfast that day?" a worried Martha Thompson said. "What is the prime minister's opinion on wheat subsidies in Saskatchewan? What are his thoughts on the Japanese occupation of Manchuria?"

Protesters from across the country, in cities and towns big and small, began to chant about the status of speeches—to the Empire Economic Council and to the Greater New Brunswick Coal and Steel Corporation—that King was planning on making next week. Others expressed frustration about not knowing whether he'd walked his dog Pat.

By evening, the prime minister had called for calm. He apologized for causing such panic, saying that he'll compensate by making a particularly long entry about his interactions with the Hungarian ambassador today, along with details about the Ovaltine industry.

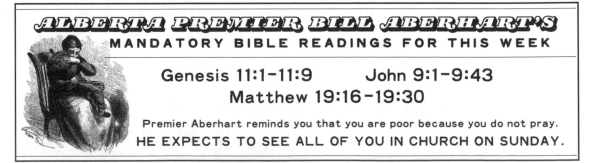

# King Meets Hitler

*In 1937, Prime Minister Mackenzie King met with German Chancellor Adolf Hitler. King's subsequent diary entry shines a light on the great machinations of his international diplomacy.*

——— JUNE 29, 1937 ———

After conversing with Goering for two hours about the similarities between Germany and Canada, I was directed to enter the room where Herr Hitler was to receive me. When the doors opened, I saw the Chancellor wearing an evening uniform. He greeted me with a warm handshake and we sat down in comfortable chairs with the translator seated between us. Given the recent militarization of Europe and the rise of fascist governments, I provided him with a gift that is sure to calm things down: a deluxe copy of my biography, written by one of my Cabinet ministers, Norman Rogers.

I opened it for him and presented the photos of my childhood in Berlin, Ontario, which shares the same name as the German capital. And it's no coincidence that Berlin, Ontario, has a strong German heritage. I could tell he took great interest in Canada's German's connections—he kept talking about how vital those people would be for the next thousand years.

We discussed, at some length, the remilitarization of the Rhineland. Hitler said that it was part of his overall plan for world domination. He expressed his desire to create an Aryan master race and his intention to one day wipe out the Jewish race. I replied that one of Canada's main exports was wheat, which is a main ingredient in German beer.

> "I provided him with a gift that is sure to calm things down: a deluxe copy of my biography, written by one of my Cabinet ministers, Norman Rogers," writes PM Mackenzie King

He then informed me that he intended to kill millions of people and obliterate any nation that doesn't stand behind the Third Reich. I told him there are many towns in Ontario that still celebrate Oktoberfest. The Nazi leader remarked that the worst was yet to come in an inevitable global conflict. That's when I knew I had to speak up and firmly remind him of Steinbach, Manitoba, a friendly place that had thousands of German-speaking people.

After our hour-and-a-half talk, I thanked the Chancellor for his time and returned to the hotel. Hitler is a bit misguided with his somewhat dangerous plans, but he is a passionate man who truly loves his people. I hope he enjoys reading my biography.

## 1937 CBC Radio Schedule

*The Canadian Broadcasting Corporation presents the nation's finest and only radio shows in the country*

—

### TODAY'S PROGRAMMING

11:00 A.M.—News from the Colonies

11:30 A.M.—S'well Chipper Chap Super Happy Gang Valium Hour

12:30 P.M.—Wheat Farm Silo Report

1:30 P.M.—This Hour has 22 Doukhobors

2:30 P.M.—Time Signal's Short Dash Followed by Long Dash

4:00 P.M.—The Maple Leaf Forever (verses 1–4)

5:15 P.M.—Enunciation Tonight with J. Frank Willis

6:00 P.M.—God Save the King

7:00 P.M.—The Horse Sport Report with Mort

7:45 P.M.—Static and Garbled Transmissions from Afar

11:00 P.M.—Sign off.

# WAR? MAYBE!

*"North America's Trusted Source of News."*

## THE BEAVERTON

MONDAY, SEPTEMBER 4, 1939.

5¢ PER COPY 30¢ PER WEEK

INDEX

Business... B1
Lifestyle... B8
Local... C9
World... C1
Sports... D6
World... C1

**WEATHER**

*There are more important things to worry about.*

## KING SAYS COUNTRY SHOULD BE 'FASHIONABLY LATE' WITH WAR DECLARATION, DOESN'T WANT TO APPEAR DESPERATE

OTTAWA—Since Britain and France have now declared war on Germany in response to Hitler's invasion of Poland, Canada has made it clear that it could possibly be joining and most likely fighting on the side of Britain.

Thousands of men have been lining up at what many assume will become army recruiting stations. Meanwhile, children all over the country collect metal and rubber scraps so that soon-to-be-erected factories can use them to produce the munitions, tanks, and airplanes we might need. Women have been impatiently checking their wristwatches to see how long it'll be before they can show up to work in overalls and handle a blowtorch.

"I've been printing war bonds and anti-hoarding posters all morning," said Theodore Yannick of Hull, Quebec, anticipating that Prime Minister Mackenzie King will, at some point, declare a state of war with one or more countries. "I've also been censoring my own diary so that German and/or Russian spies won't have access to important details about my thoughts."

Meanwhile in Ottawa, Prime Minister King has been passing the time with small chores such as a fixing a loose chair leg, reviewing his diaries, and rereading *War and Peace.*

"If we are to join this war, we have to wait a few days so that people won't think we're doing this just because Britain did," said King to Parliament during a special-session debate. "It's a social faux pas to be exactly on time for a war. We don't want to appear desperate—so let's procrastinate a bit longer and see where it goes."

*P.M. William Lyon Mackenzie King plays it cool, waits for phone to ring.*

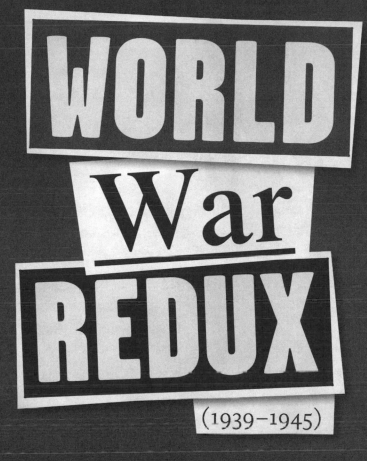

# WORLD War REDUX

## (1939–1945)

"Fuck." —Adolf Hitler, 1945

Our boys in uniform bravely fought in all four corners of the globe. Our girls at home bravely picked up the slack in the armaments and munitions factories. And our government bravely interned Japanese Canadians and refused to accept Jewish refugees. Truly, this was the Greatest Generation.

# KEY DATES

September 3, 1939
Second World War begins

September 10, 1939
Canada remembers it forgot to
respond to Britain's invitation

December 7, 1941
Canada declares war on Japan, Hungary,
and Romania; due to paperwork error,
government also declares war on Finland

March 15, 1942
22,000 Japanese Canadians
decide to move away from hustle
and bustle of Vancouver

August 14, 1943
Dieppe force links up with Russians
to liberate POW camp

September 14, 1943
Wayne and Shuster unveil secret shtick
to win war with Hitler impersonation

April 18, 1944
Unstoppable Dieppe forces
take Rome, eye Tokyo

June 6, 1944
14,000 Canadian troops seize Juno
Beach in D-Day campaign that will
ultimately lead to Hitler's defeat and
future generations' feelings of inferiority

August 14, 1945
Invincible Dieppe forces liberate
China, conquer Japan

# Mackenzie King's Thoughts on the Eve of War

*Mackenzie King had many advisers, including those in the spiritual realm, who helped him make such difficult decisions as whether to declare war on Germany.*

—————— SEPTEMBER 8, 1939 ——————

Had a restless sleep last night. Upon emerging from my slumber, my thoughts turned to whether I should wake up or continue sleeping. Unable to arrive at a conclusion, I decided to defer the matter and stared at the ceiling for 90 minutes.

I needed to speak with Pat and Grandmama about whether Canada, free to make its own foreign policy decisions since 1931, ought to aid Britain by entering the war. I knew I'd have to get Wilfrid's take as well, since if I didn't he would insist anyway.

I sat down at the séance around 3:00. Grandmama was adamant that no matter what I did, it was vital to factor in the interests and perceptions of the Americans in the declaration, and to make sure that in our actions we did nothing to impinge upon their neutrality—staying on their good side will come in handy if we wish to eventually bring them in on our side. She also offered that eternity was treating the family well, and they all looked forward to seeing me.

Wilfrid agreed, noting it was important not to emphasize our allegiance to Britain too much lest it alienate French Canada. I would have to be careful to make sure Quebec voters understood that we were fighting for the basic, broadest tenets of freedom and democracy and not just out of blind allegiance to an English-speaking Crown.

Pat, however, offered the most useful advice. After barking for a minute or two and asking for a belly rub, he noted that while I would have to craft the text of the declaration, the actual measures taken to engage in the war could be decided in Parliament. Therefore, the extent of Canada's participation and the decisions I'd have to make would be limited.

With all three of my trusted advisers in unison, my decision was made. Tomorrow, we declare war on Germany.

---

### IN THE NEWS

Germany formally surrenders, marking last time Western world will have to worry about Nazis

---

Married soldier who brought home Dutch woman to waiting wife inspires new situational comedy show

---

# Freedom of speech saved after Montreal mayor imprisoned for expressing opinion

—————— AUGUST 7, 1940 ——————

MONTREAL — Montreal mayor Camillien Houde was promptly arrested yesterday for expressing views contrary to the Allies' fight to save democratic societies from Hitler's armies.

"We are trying to defeat the tyranny and fascism that enforce unflinching loyalty to the state," said Justice Minister Lapointe outside the police station where a shackled Houde was being interrogated. "Mayor Houde refused to carry out the instructions as prescribed."

Three days earlier, in an apparent violation of the War Measures Act, the controversial mayor spoke out against the mandatory registration of all men for conscription. Lapointe noted that the subsequent arrest and imprisonment of Mayor Houde without trial was a necessary step in preventing the forces of oppression and tyranny from winning the war.

Houde has been removed from his post as mayor and carted away to an internment camp, where he will remain for the duration of the war.

# King slightly concerned after not having heard from Hong Kong force in months

*Ill-prepared soldiers sent to defend island from Japanese have yet to send PM a Christmas card*

—————— APRIL 2, 1942 ——————

OTTAWA — The prime minister and his Cabinet are somewhat troubled after not hearing from the two thousand Canadian troops sent to protect Hong Kong against the onslaught of the Japanese war machine. They never even mailed a Christmas card.

"They're probably just busy with all the fun they must be having right now," King told reporters on Parliament Hill. "Or maybe they've been distracted by the local girls, if you know what I mean."

> "No news must be good news."
> — Defence Minister Ralston

Defence Minister James Ralston added that he suspected the delay has more to do with their receiving the long-delayed shipment of supplies the government had finally gotten around to sending them. "No news must be good news." The Canadian government is planning on sending an envoy to check on the troops, just as soon as they've finished their plan to invade Nazi-occupied France all on their own.

# The Canadian Corvette

*The Flower-class Corvette was responsible for protecting merchant ships from U-boat attacks.*

**SONAR:** Emits Benny Goodman's version of "Sing, Sing, Sing" to detect U-boats sending a terrifyingly jazzy chill up the spines of German crews below

**Surfaces for ice to build up on:** able to disguise ship as iceberg if it doesn't capsize first

**Crew quarters:** Complete with a cozy one square centimetre for each crew member

**Bridge:** Left open to elements so that captain may beseech Poseidon directly

**HF/DF antenna:** Intercepts U-boat radio transmissions to catch up on all the gossip, such as what Grand Admiral Donitz was wearing at the last Nazi parade

**Engine:** Capable of speeds of up to 16 knots, ensuring that ship is pushed backward by only 48% of waves

**Puke deck:** Sadly, located below the poop deck

**Depth charges:** Explosive fish-killing barrels

# Alaskan Highway construction delayed by slow-moving motorhome

*Swiss tourists taking in sights of Northern Canada moving at 5 mph*

—————— JUNE 14, 1942 ——————

WHITEHORSE — Soldiers of the U.S. Army Corps of Engineers attempting to widen the Alaskan Highway have been significantly delayed by two Swiss retirees in a large recreational vehicle who are refusing to drive faster than five miles per hour.

"Holy shit," muttered one American soldier, his bulldozer crawling behind the massive land ship. "And he's not even pulling over to let me pass."

Hans and Noémie Müller's vehicle has been occupying the single lane for hours now, interfering with the troops' attempt to complete a supply line from Dawson Creek, B.C., to the Delta Junction, Alaska, in order to deter a possible Japanese invasion.

A long line of supply trucks and construction equipment followed in the path of the curious couple, who have always wanted to drive across Canada and the U.S.

"Please move so we can finish laying the gravel!" yelled Private Harold Dent over a bullhorn. "Uh . . . bitte moven sie so wir finishen der gravel."

According to sources, progress on the Alaskan Highway then came to a complete stop after the Müllers thought they saw a black bear.

# "Get me a Nazi paratrooper combat knife or don't come back, Dad!"

## Navy mixologists unveil sophisticated new "rum and Coke" cocktail

———— OCTOBER 1, 1941 ————

HALIFAX — The Royal Canadian Navy has issued new equipment that officials say makes our sailors at least twice as combat effective.

The new standard-issue cocktail was introduced after navy officers gave high ratings to prototypes that made the daily rum ration "smoother."

Chemists at the RCN laboratories report that they'd made numerous failed attempts, having tried tonic water, club soda, tomato juice, and condensed milk.

Rear Admiral Percy Nelles said it was a proud day for the navy, adding, "Whereas before we had to fully and completely taste the alcohol, causing frequent burning, coughing, and teary eyes, now Canadian seamen can safely and effectively imbibe and recover in half the time, buying us precious seconds of improved proficiency under enemy fire."

According to the *RCN Field Manual*, First Edition, the drink is made out of one ounce Captain Morgan rum to at least one part Coca-Cola, although two parts Coca-Cola were often recommended in order to get the ideal "forgetting you're drinking alcohol" experience.

Back at home, army scientists say they've found a way to make use of the excess rye and ginger ale they've been given.

## Japanese-Canadian Great War vet granted internment camp honour

——— MARCH 16, 1942 ———

VANCOUVER — A veteran of the Great War has received the honour of being declared an enemy of the state and offered free housing and a trip to the interior thanks to his Japanese heritage.

Steve Harada, who served in the Canadian Expeditionary Force and was wounded twice, had never received any veteran benefits for his bravery until now.

"I nearly died for this country and this is the recognition I get?" yelled Harada as an RCMP officer pushed him and his family onto a waiting train headed for Taber, Alberta. "I am a loyal Canadian citizen born in Vancouver!"

While interned, Harada and

the rest of his family will be retrained as sugar beet farmers so that they never have to return to the West Coast. The free shack accommodations feature a single woodstove and floorboard beds.

At press time, four-year-old Tim Watanabe was suspected of leading an elaborate spy ring that directed Japanese bombers during the attack on Pearl Harbor last year.

# King buying time on restaurant menu choice: "Soup if necessary, but not necessarily soup"

——— APRIL 24, 1942 ———

OTTAWA — After spending three hours analyzing every detail of the menu at Betty's Café in downtown Ottawa, Prime Minister Mackenzie King has refused to take a firm position on what he'll be ordering for lunch.

Trying to take his mind off whether to implement conscription through a plebiscite, King thoroughly reviewed the options with his waitress, Cheryl LaPierre. He asked nearly every question possible, including what province the food came from, the nutritional value of

the whipped cream on the ice cream sundae, whether they were using Ontario peameal bacon, and how much the deluxe burger cost, after tax.

"It's true that I'm hungry and need a source of energy to sustain my life by consuming food," babbled King to the confused and frustrated diner patrons. "Let's start with the drinks. I could order a five-cent coffee or tea. There are also milkshakes sold at this establishment, but that type of beverage could also be ordered exclusively as a dessert option."

After 45 minutes, King made his first decision: he would not

be ordering from the child's menu. However, King remained coy on whether he'd be ordering a starter for the table or going directly to the main course.

"How would Quebec respond if I ordered the steak rather than the tourtière?" wondered King to his exhausted waitress. "We must observe these national sensitivities, even in the slightest. My decision must be rigorously tested under every circumstance."

Ultimately, King decided to hold a referendum in the restaurant next week on whether he'd be ordering the soup or the salad.

# Janowski RCMP Report

*German spy Werner von Janowski was caught a day after landing in Canada. The RCMP, amateurs in international espionage, attempted to turn Janowski into a double agent. However, Janowski took advantage of their trust in his counter-intelligence reports, feeding them false information.*

JANOWSKI, WERNER VON

**ROYAL CANADIAN MOUNTED POLICE**

DIVISION  SUB-DIVISION  DETACHMENT

PROVINCE
NEW BRUNSWICK

DATE
April 15, 1943.

FILE REFERENCES
TOP SECRET

RE:  OPERATION WATCHDOG
Attn : Stuart Wood

14-4-43.

1.     A German agent has placed a very secret message attached to the leg of a brooding Canada Goose in a flock of 200 in a Moncton, New Brunswick, city park. This message must be intercepted if there is any hope of capturing U-518 and the spies on board.

2.     The message is only half of the transmission. The other half can only be intercepted by tuning into tonight's radio broadcast of Little Orphan Annie—brought to you by Ovaltine. Pay attention at the end of the show where a secret code will be read. Make sure you have your Little Orphan Annie secret decoding badge on hand to translate the code and be sure to drink your Ovaltine.

3.     Combine the two messages and relay it back to Hamburg, using my specially designed wooden transmitter, so that U-518 will be given the go ahead to surface in Lake Winnipeg near Gimli where it can be promptly captured.

AGENT "BOBBY" JANOWSKI

RECEIVED

HEADQUARTERS

SUB-DIVISION

DETACHMENT

P.C.R.

A. R. V. NO.

DIARY DATE

SET FOR

# Ukrainians happy not to be interned in this war

———— JULY 16, 1943 ————

REGINA — Canada's Ukrainian community was relieved to find out that they will not be forced into labour camps for the duration of the war, unlike as with the previous war with Germany.

"When I heard the news that Canada was involved in another war, I lined up at the nearest police station to be interned," said Petro Tereshchenko, a Ukrainian-born Canadian citizen who was interned for four years at a labour camp in Alberta during the Great War. "But then nothing happened. I have been waiting for three years for a military truck to come by, place me in an isolated camp, and force me to build roads for 25 cents a day, but I'm still here."

Nor has any community member been declared an "enemy alien," had their wealth confiscated, or been required to carry identity papers.

"It's good that my circumstance of birth puts me on the Allied side," added Tereshchenko.

# Canadians land at Dieppe, take Paris

*No casualties reported*

———— AUGUST 20, 1942 ————

LONDON — Combined Operations Headquarters confirmed that after successfully landing at the French port of Dieppe, the Canadian Armed Forces have taken Paris.

"Oh yeah, they did great," stammered one heavily perspiring official. "No casualties whatsoever. The force will remain in Paris until we can provide additional support."

According to a briefing given by Canadian Military Headquarters public relations officers as they ran through a fire exit, Canadian forces supported by British, American, and Free French commandos stormed the beaches of the heavily fortified port town of Dieppe on the morning of the 19th, obliterating the defenders and subsequently storming 120 miles on foot to liberate the French capital.

A public relations officer further stated: "Everything went according to plan, especially the part when all the German machine guns and rifles jammed, giving our brave fighting men time to get on shore, take thousands of prisoners, and liberate Paris."

When approached for comment, Defence Minister Ralston raised his index finger as if he were about to say something, then abruptly turned and darted out of the room.

Government officials are already calling this the most successful Canadian mission since Canadian paratroopers stormed Berlin in 1938, killing Hitler and preventing the war before it ever happened.

# Gonorrhea launches invasion of Italy with Canadian support

———— SEPTEMBER 3, 1943 ————

SICILY — In a bid to strike at the soft underbelly of Nazi tyranny, the venereal disease known as gonorrhea launched an amphibious assault on Sicily yesterday, aided by the courage and sexual stamina of our Canadian armed forces.

"We're just doing what we can to serve our country," said infantryman Connor McCutcheon. "And it's an honour to take part in a mission as important, and frankly, fun, as this one."

Sources report that the disease made landfall on the south coast of Sicily early in the morning. Its forces faced little resistance as it worked its way up toward the urinary tract of the Italian peninsula.

Though combat has only just begun, the Canadians are already earning themselves a reputation as "shock troops," advancing the disease past formidable defences such as machine gun nests, fortified hilltop artillery, and protective Italian fathers.

> "It's an honour to take part in a mission as important, and frankly, fun, as this one."
> — Connor McCutcheon

"I think we were well prepared for this encounter after the failed syphilis invasion of France back in '42," McCutcheon stated.

# Am I Aiding the Enemy?

*By Constance*

———— OCTOBER 22, 1943 ————

Once again it's Wednesday, and Constance is back to answer your questions on the little things you can do to be less treasonous and more supportive of our boys at the front. Our first letter:

—

*Dear Constance,*
   *My neighbour keeps complaining that my rose garden is going over the property line and spreading onto his lawn. I don't think it's that big a deal, but I just want to make sure: am I aiding fascist tyranny?*

   *Sincerely,*
   *An Unassured Gardener*

Dear Unassured,
   Whoa, hold on there! Roses? Let me answer your question with another question. Can a squad, a regiment, or a division fuel themselves with roses? When you're sitting in a foxhole covered in your own filth, looking to grab a single ounce of nourishment in the only five minutes of peace you have between bombardments, do you take out your bayonet and crack open a tin of roses? You'd best rip out those treasonous flowers and put in some vegetables. And buy some Victory Bonds.

—

*Dear Constance,*
   *Yesterday, I came home from the ordnance factory and told my husband I was tired because I had to spend all day fixing a machine that had broken down. Now I'm worried because I just saw a poster that says loose lips sink ships. How many ships have I sunk?*
   *Regards,*
   *A Concerned Armourer*

Dear Concerned,
   It's impossible to say for certain how many ships your careless talk has sent to the bottom of the North Atlantic. Just off the top of my head, I'll say five. But to really gauge the true extent of your betrayal, you need to answer some questions. First, has your husband ever lapsed into German? Second, have you found any radio transmitters around the house that you did not purchase yourself? Third, does he keep a stiletto with a swastika on the handle in the drawer next to the bed? If the answer to any of these questions is yes, then you both deserve to be executed. However, your sentence may be reduced if you buy some Victory Bonds, which I recommend doing as a precautionary measure.

—

Those are our questions for this week. If you think you might be undermining the Allied cause, write Constance at:

Constance Jenkins
c/o *The Beaverton*
603 Markham St.
Toronto 4, Ontario

# RCAF bombers obliterate cabbage farm near German factory

———— NOVEMBER 3, 1943 ————

YORKSHIRE, ENGLAND — RCAF bombers from No. 6 Group Bomber Command have destroyed a Nazi cabbage farm roughly 10 miles from a ball-bearing factory in the Ruhr Valley.
   "I can advise that over 700 Lancaster and Halifax bombers from 420, 431, and 434 Squadrons took part in the mission last night," said RCAF Group Captain Walter Moore. "Together they successfully annihilated Hitler's mighty vegetable production machine.
   "And we lost only 234 of our aircrew!" Moore added.
   With pinpoint accuracy, the boys of Bomber Command struck at the heart of the four-mile-long field that may have been producing the mighty leafy-green plant. The cabbage field, which intelligence officers speculate could have one day become a factory, airfield, or beet-production facility, is now no longer usable.
   Air Marshall Sir Arthur Harris explained: "Victory is near. The German people will never be able to survive without their beloved cabbage rolls."

# Pair of breasts drawn on plane inspires air crews

———— NOVEMBER 3, 1943 ————

HALIFAX —When they're not bombing Jerry at night, Crew 43 of 434 Squadron RCAF Bomber Command spend most of their time expressing their artistic talents by painting tits on their Lancaster bomber.

The plane, called *Titania* after the Queen of the Fairies in Shakespeare's play *A Midsummer Night's Dream*, features two supple, round breasts with soft, not-too-big nipples designed on the nose.

"I was inspired by Botticelli's *Birth of Venus*," said navigator F/O Frank McGeorge from Toronto, who helped draw the outline of the flawless areolas and erect nipples. "And my work has been influenced by Eugène

Delacroix's *Liberty Leading the People*. It's quite a masterpiece that I hope all the 19- to 22-year-old air crews can enjoy."

McGeorge has added his practised boob depictions to other objects as well, including his flight jacket, maps, target tokens, the mess hall, the runway, and the squadron's executive officer's staff car.

"Hey, look at these perfect jugs!" pilot F/Sgt. Jean "Esky" Escaravage exclaimed, captivated by nipples that resembled headlights. "This guy has talent."

McGeorge and Escavage are confident that German flak crews and night fighter pilots will be too distracted appreciating the set of knockers on their plane to shoot back.

# Unpatriotic baby born with flat feet

———— JANUARY 7, 1944 ————

SHEDIAC, N.B. — Three-day-old Ian Menard has already let down the country by choosing to be born without any arches in his feet, thereby disqualifying him for future service in Canada's army.

A doctor at a local New Brunswick hospital made the seditious discovery during a routine check after childbirth.

"It's always hard to tell a mother that her child was born a nine-and-a-half-pound coward," said Dr. Bert Mallick. "The fetus was most likely exposed to pacifism and fear of freedom in the first trimester. That's when flat feet and heart murmurs set in."

The tiny infant is already being investigated by RCMP for being a most adorable Nazi sympathizer.

# Military historians storm Normandy to bear witness

——— JUNE 6, 1944 ———

NORMANDY, FRANCE — A force of 10,000 middle-aged white male historians representing the U.S., Britain, and Canada have successfully landed on the designated beaches of Omaha, Utah, Gold, Sword, and Juno in Normandy in order to witness, interpret, and analyze the greatest day in military history.

Early reports indicate that the German coastal defences have been all but destroyed by the soldiers, airmen, and sailors of the Allied Forces. Meanwhile, tenured professors and postdoctoral fellows have begun a full frontal assault of theses, papers, and archives on the subject of modern warfare.

The previous night, hundreds

of history graduate students were parachuted in behind enemy lines to reinforce the academy and embed themselves. No matter what the enemy threw at them, they refused to stop reading.

"I've waited my entire career for something like this to happen," explained Dr. Gregory Flambolt of McGill, bullets zipping by his head as he wrote about what he was seeing on Juno Beach. "I've studied amphibious assaults from ancient Greece to Gallipoli, but none like this one. We're here to ensure that our soldiers understand the significance of what they're doing on this day."

By H-Hour +6 the teachers and researchers had made progress on discourse, achieving consensus that the beachhead

would have some significance on the war's outcome but remaining unclear as to whether Germany's war industry could sustain itself fighting on three fronts and whether the Atlantic Wall had been completed prior to the invasion.

"We're still waiting to receive, translate, and compare Rommel's journal entry with testimony from slave labourers and the Czechoslovakian conscripts who were used to defend the beach," noted Professor H.M. Miller of Royal Military College.

However, the greatest day for war historians came at a cost: heavy arguments and contrary interpretations left hundreds with bruised egos, unfinished papers, and broken tenure tracks.

# Military brass say all the good operation names already taken

————— FEBRUARY 2, 1945 —————

ANTWERP — Senior Allied commanders are reporting that all the badass-sounding operation code names have now been claimed.

"Overlord, Totality, Husky—these are handles that men will sacrifice themselves for, and they really make Jerry shake in his boots," said Field Marshal Montgomery as he looked over maps from his headquarters in a bombed-out chateau. "But how am I supposed to get my troops motivated for Operation Teakettle?"

In the course of the struggle against Nazi Germany, Supreme Headquarters Allied Expedi-

tionary Force (SHAEF) has led millions of actions and exercises, some as small as a single orderly getting an important message from one HQ to another and others amounting to massive campaigns requiring the coordination of multitudes. As a result, they've run out of nouns that are appropriately intimidating.

"First we tried looking at planets, stars, and constellations," said American General Omar Bradley. "But of course those had all been used. We looked for animals next, but it turns out they were some of the first to go. So now I have to tell my troops to ready themselves because Operation Overlord IV:

This Time It's Personal kicks off at 0900 tomorrow."

According to many in the field, the problem is only getting worse as the war drags on, with the crumbling Third Reich still refusing to capitulate.

"We're at our wits' end," admitted Canadian Lieutenant-General Guy Simonds. "Yesterday I had to write 150 wives and mothers that their loved ones didn't return from Operation Operation, and now I have to tell the boys that tomorrow's leave is cancelled yet again because if Operation Wet Wipes doesn't go ahead ASAP, the cloud cover will take away our air support. When will this war finally end?"

# MOVEMBRANCE DAY HONOURS

In homage to the mighty, virile men who fought valiantly with their bushy follicular upper lips pressed firmly in the direction of the enemy, we salute you and everything those waxed 'stached faces stood for. Whether it was a handlebar, a duster, or even a Fu-Manchu, these Canadians knew the power of face fuzz.

# After hard night celebrating VE Day, nation wakes up with several cold sores

———— MAY 9, 1945 ————

HALIFAX — Millions of haggard but happy Canadians were surprised to wake up to blisters and sores around their lips after embracing fellow citizens to mark the end of the war.

"I knew I shouldn't have kissed all those sailors!" said a visibly upset Marie LaMay while trying to mask her orofacial infection with makeup. "I'm getting married tomorrow! How could this happen to me?"

Over 5 million Canadians celebrating the victory over Nazism and tyranny were soon regretting bracing lips with countless strangers. Doctors speculate that the outbreak can be traced to a Fredericton milkman named Dave who had an open sore on his lip and smooched every woman, man, and child without considering how rapidly the virus would spread.

"It was just an innocent peck from four dozen or so people," explained Merv Williams, an RCAF fighter pilot who returned home a few weeks ago from his tour of duty. "I didn't pay any attention to what they looked like or whether they wanted it. It was the heat of the moment."

At press time, the nation completely forgot it was still at war with Japan.

INDEX

Business ..... B7
Lifestyle ..... B1
Local ..... C1

Politics ..... A1
Sports ..... D1
World ..... G1

"North America's Trusted Source of News."

# THE BEAVERTON

TUESDAY, OCTOBER 16, 1945.

WEATHER
Cloudy with 30% chance of nuclear annihilation.

6¢ PER COPY 55¢ PER WEEK

# BABY BONUS WILL CREATE LAZY BABIES WHO SHOULD BE WORKING FOR FAMILIES INSTEAD

### Alvin McTavish

OTTAWA—Our federal government's new plan to give $5 to each child per week subsidizes laziness and sloth among our infants. Why are we subsidizing children? Just so they can eat, sleep, poop, and cry? That's not how modern economies are built and it's not how we beat the Nazis.

Back in my day, we were required to do chores immediately after being born. In fact, I had to help raise two barns, all five fields, and milk the cows while still dripping with my mother's placenta. There was always work to be done and I didn't wait around for some doctor to snip my umbilical cord; I did it myself. I wasn't yet able to hold up my own head, but I didn't complain. My family of 267 never received any kind of bonus luxury, so why should this generation?

The moment we begin subsidizing babies they'll begin asking for cars, property, and basic public education. Should we start paying for every child's medical bills simply because they catch a little polio? Walk it off, I say.

# Booms

## Atomic, Baby, and

# OTHERWISE

### (1945–1966)

"I am a Canadian. Free to speak without fear, free to stand for what I think right, free to oppose what I believe wrong, and free to choose those who shall govern my country. Also I hate Americans" —John Diefenbaker

Waking up from the hangover of another World War victory, Canada had earned a place in the world by not being an utterly devastated European country ridden with shell holes. It was a time of peace, but also one of worry. So how did Canadians cope with the stress of the Cold War and the ongoing threat of nuclear annihilation? They made babies. A lot of babies. Good thing, too, because having a large car and a house in the suburbs along with at least six children was mandated by the government.

# KEY DATES

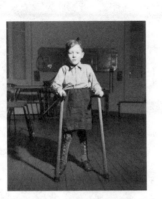

**December 20, 1952**
*Elderly Uncle* magazine chooses
Prime Minister Louis St. Laurent
as Uncle of the Year

**May 8, 1956**
0% of Canadian parents refuse
to give their child the polio
vaccination over fears of autism

**June 20, 1959**
The Great Hula Hoop Disaster

**January 24, 1960**
Diefenbaker government
outlaws Hula Hoops

**May 4, 1963**
Hula Hoops legal again after
added safety measures

# Women carry munitions production back into domestic sphere

## IN THE NEWS

Amazing: New Canadian home made entirely out of asbestos

New queen, Elizabeth II, promises 50% more royal waves, stylish hats

CBC's Friendly Giant accidentally crushes five

How to get your children to stop asking about the war

First nuclear reactor in Canada causes politicians to glow

Flames extinguished from piano keys after Oscar Peterson finishes

# Movie interrupted by loud civil rights violation

———— NOVEMBER 9, 1946 ————

NEW GLASGOW, NS — A showing of *The Dark Mirror* at the Roseland Film Theatre was rudely interrupted last night by a loud act of discrimination.

Moviegoers at the opening night of the thriller directed by Robert Siodmak and starring Olivia de Havilland couldn't help but be distracted by a coloured woman who refused to follow the unwritten segregation rules.

"Shhhhh!" sounded one member of the audience after being annoyed by the confrontation developing near the front row.

Important dialogue and

scenes were missed because of the repeated disturbances.

"Some of us are trying to watch the movie!" scorned another to the coloured woman who was arguing with the theatre manager. "Could you please make these civil rights protests outside in the lobby?"

Despite repeated calls to quiet down, the noise continued to rise, especially when a policeman forcibly removed the woman, causing injury to her hip.

"You know, she really ruined the whole showing and I'll be forced to pay another 40 cents to see it again," one man explained to the press after the movie was finished. "My rights as a moviegoer were clearly violated."

# The Gouzenko Archives

Igor Gouzenko was the renowned Soviet spy turned informant known for kicking off the Cold War in Canada with his defection in 1945. Famous for never revealing his face, little is known about Gouzenko beyond his shocking revelation. However, in scouring archives in Canada and the former Soviet Union for material relating to Gouzenko's youth, we unearthed the following photographs from Igor's childhood, adolescence, and adulthood. Together they provide a visual history of the man behind the mask.

Igor as a child: Rogachov, USSR, 1923.

Eighth birthday party (Igor's the one holding the cake), circa 1927.

As a teenager on holiday in Seliger Lake, near Ostashkov in Central USSR, circa 1937.

Documentation given to Gouzenko upon joining the military at the start of the Second World War.

Here with his favourite book in 1953, Ottawa.

# Tommy Douglas Speech: "And by 'Eugenics' I Meant 'Universal Health Care'"

——— JULY 12, 1947 ———

*In 1947, beloved Canadian Tommy Douglas gave a speech intended to clarify what some saw as his controversial position on eugenics: the pseudoscience, popular with Nazis, which holds that it's possible to improve the genetic makeup of the human population. The transcript of his speech follows.*

—

Friends,

I thought I'd take this opportunity to clarify what I've written and said in regard to the field of eugenics.

Some of you may recall a fable I told about separating all the mentally defective mice from the normal mice population so as not to place a burden on mouse society. Others may recall a prairie-themed tale about subnormal people filled with lax morality, venereal diseases, and low intelligence who shouldn't be trusted with a milk separator and should instead be sent to state farms where they can more effectively contribute to society.

Those were not, as some of my critics have claimed, euphemisms for eugenics. I was actually making a complicated parallel about what we can achieve together: universal health care.

My fellow Canadians, I can assure you that the master's thesis I wrote entitled "The Problems of the Subnormal Family" was not about creating a master race, but about the problems many Canadian families face in trying to receive medical treatment. You don't need to read it; I can assure you that it's long and dull.

> "Those were not, as some of my critics have claimed, euphemisms for eugenics."

A responsible state should ensure that all its citizens, regardless of race, gender, class, creed, or disability, have access to free health care, just like how B.C. and Alberta provide free forced sterilizations and institutionalization of those deemed mentally handicapped. Of course I've never, nor will ever, endorse such a dehumanizing practice as sterilizing and imprisoning someone just because they're different. The important thing is that they get these services free of charge.

Furthermore, we must ensure that the cost of health care never threatens to bankrupt good, hardworking, genetically superior Canadians. Otherwise, how will they ever find the time to breed?

To sum up, my point is this: Medicare is something I've been fighting for my entire life, and that's how you'll remember me.

# Nature hinders progress on Leduc oil development

*Alberta government calls for the phasing out of all trees, rivers*

——— SEPTEMBER 15, 1947 ———

EDMONTON — One day after striking oil at Leduc #1, the brave men of Imperial Oil are still fighting Mother Nature as she continues to stand in the way of the company's further exploitation of Alberta's oil and gas fields.

Trees, plants, rivers, and some animal life remain atop what may be one of the world's largest sources of crude oil, demonstrating no regard for Alberta's and Canada's future economic growth.

"Nature threw everything at us, but we managed to find where she was hiding the oil," said one worker. "Unfortunately, there's a lot of vegetation in the way of future wells we're intending to drill. We need the government to act to eliminate this needless organic greenery that obstructs development."

Alberta premier Ernest Manning has promised to cut down, dig up, and burn away any form of life that even crosses the path of oil equipment.

If nature refuses to comply, the province may have to resort to the same drastic measures it used to kick Aboriginal tribes off the land several years ago.

## Women's Sphere Magazine

*The Toronto-based* Women's Sphere *magazine ran from 1946 to 1972. The publication focused on modern women trying to balance their lives between supporting their husbands' careers and taking care of the children.*

**WOMEN'S SPHERE** 10 CENTS NOVEMBER 1946

FEATURING ● THE HOME: YOUR *NATURAL* HABITAT
12 DIFFERENT SMILES TO BRIGHTEN YOUR HUSBAND'S DAY
WHAT'S WRONG WITH MY BODY? WE ASK A GROUP OF MALE DOCTORS

**WOMEN'S SPHERE** AUGUST 1948

**TOO SKINNY?**
Gain At Least 10 Pounds with This All-Butter Diet
**FRIGIDAIRE FRIDGES:** Freon Is Your Friend
**10 TIPS** on Making Your Sensitive Son
Look LE$S HOMOSEXUAL
How to Apply *YOUR* Post-Secondary Education
While Cleaning *YOUR* Washroom

BUTTER
FROZEN BUTTER

# Newfoundland joins Canada 30 minutes earlier than expected

—— MARCH 31, 1949 ——

ST. JOHN'S — Canadians across the country were shocked to find Newfoundland already celebrating its status as a province at 10:30 p.m. Eastern Standard time.

"I don't get it. What's the deal with the half hour?" Eloise Orchard asked at her Confederation party. "Is it an April Fool's joke? If so, they're early."

Confusion has run rampant from the now coast-to-coast nation about how this will affect day-to-day proceedings.

"What does that mean for radio programs?" asked John Clifton in Toronto. "Do they get the news on the hour or the half hour? Are they ahead or behind? Maybe this whole thing wasn't worth it and we should have just left them out."

The new province has raised questions about the role of time zones in Canadian society.

"I get that they have their own rum, language, and propensity to kiss fish in bars, but why do they get their own time zone?" asked Margaret Fillion of Quebec. "That doesn't mesh with my version of the inclusion we're trying to establish here in Canada."

A passionate two-year-old named Brian Williams from Winnipeg, however, has found this to be the best thing ever.

# The 1951 Census Report

*By 1951 Canada's population had grown by nearly 22% since 1941, when the last census was taken. Here's the federal government's brief overview.*

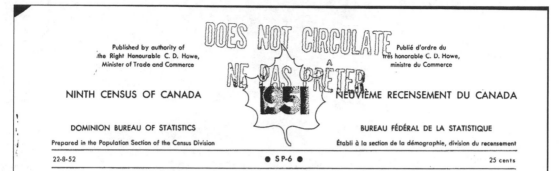

Published by authority of
the Right Honourable C. D. Howe,
Minister of Trade and Commerce

Publié d'ordre du
très honorable C. D. Howe,
ministre du Commerce

DOES NOT CIRCULATE
NE PAS PRÊTER
1951

## NINTH CENSUS OF CANADA

## NEUVIÈME RECENSEMENT DU CANADA

DOMINION BUREAU OF STATISTICS

BUREAU FÉDÉRAL DE LA STATISTIQUE

Prepared in the Population Section of the Census Division

Établi à la section de la démographie, division du recensement

22-8-52      ● SP-6 ●      25 cents

## SYNOPSIS

### by official language and mother tongue

The results of the 1951 Census have been analyzed in this report and compared with the 1941 Census. Key findings:

· 62% of children were born in a hospital, representing a 47% increase. Fewer infants were reported as being born in a ditch.

· 55% of the population preferred to smoke Camel cigarettes, 26% preferred Du Maurier, and 8% each for Marlboro and Philip Morris. This suggests Canadians prefer a tobacco smooth in taste.

· 67% of Canadians reported that they owned an automobile, and the remainder said they wished they owned an automobile.

· 80% marked their religion as "not to be discussed in polite company."

· 18% identified "swing dancing/the bop" as the greatest threat to Canada, ahead of international communism at 16%.

## SYNOPSIS

### selon la langue officielle et la langue maternelle

Les résultats du recensement de 1951 ont été analysés dans ce rapport et comparés au recensement de 1941. Conclusions principales:

· 62% des enfants sont nés dans un hôpital, ce qui représente une augmentation de 47%. Moins de nourrissons sont nés dans un fossé.

· 55% de la population préférait fumer des cigarettes Camel, 26% préférait Du Maurier et 8% chacune pour Marlboro et Philip Morris. Cela suggère que les Canadiens préfèrent un tabac doux et suave.

· 67% des Canadiens ont indiqué qu'ils possédaient une automobile et le reste a déclaré qu'ils souhaitaient qu'ils possédaient une automobile.

· 80% ont marqué leur religion comme "ne pas être discuté en bonne société".

· 18% ont identifié "Lindy hop/Le bop" comme la plus grande menace pour le Canada, avant le communisme international à 16%.

## South Korean leader sacrifices political prisoners to honour Canada's war contributions

—————— APRIL 29, 1951 ——————

SEOUL — The Republic of Korea's president, Syngman Rhee, has executed a number of political opponents in order to honour the sacrifices made by Canadian soldiers fighting communist forces in his country.

Rhee ordered the execution of 20 leftist politicians and supporters currently being held in prison in a show of appreciation for the professionalism and bravery of the Canadian men who fought for his nation's freedom during a battle at Kapyong.

"We are very impressed with the Canadians, who held on to their positions as ferociously as I hold on to power," Rhee said in a statement to the international press. "They didn't quit and surrender, unlike these communist prisoners who have accused me of being corrupt and demanded a free and transparent election."

Canadian soldiers, sailors, and airmen have been serving in the UN-mandated police action in Korea in order to keep communism at bay and protect the Korean people's right to be ruled by a Western-friendly dictator.

The soldiers advised that they appreciated the gesture, although a nice parade or park bench dedication would have been fine.

# Sand safe after Suez peacekeeping mission

—————— NOVEMBER 28, 1956 ——————

OTTAWA — Canadian peacekeepers who've been in Egypt since the start of the month have officially reported that, thanks to their efforts, the Suez sand is safe.

"The United Nations Emergency Force has established itself within the region, and all the sand that was here previously remains in its original location," claimed Lieutenant-General E.L.M. Burns, the Canadian in charge of the force. "Once the Israeli, British, and French forces were out of the area, we were able to account for every grain of sand along the canal. A detailed 658-page report has been submitted to the UN for its approval."

Initially, the Egyptian move to control the sand within the Suez Canal region drew the concern of the British government, which had seen itself as the overseer of good sand maintenance.

"Sand might feel great between the toes when you're strolling on a beach, but that doesn't mean you can just walk up and take it," said Lester B. Pearson, secretary of state for external affairs and mastermind behind the UN's effort to send in non-combat personnel.

Pearson's plan called for a Canadian-led force to enter the region and lie down on the sand, thus preventing any of the belligerent nations from accessing it.

Already there is talk of Pearson's being awarded the Nobel Peace Prize as well as the *McTavish Sand Lovers* magazine "Sandie of the Year" award.

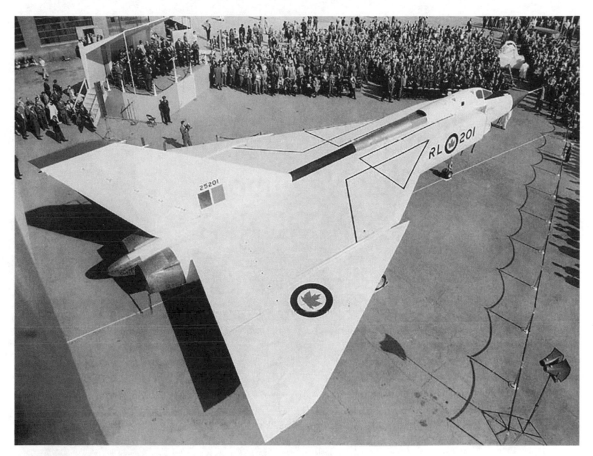

# Diefenbaker cancels Arrow program after discovering aircraft lacks cup holder

FEBRUARY 20, 1959

WINNIPEG — Prime Minister John Diefenbaker has ordered makers of Canada's most advanced interceptor to cease production after noticing that the aircraft was without cup holder capability.

"Where the hell is it?" asked the prime minister as he looked to place his "Dief the Chief" coffee mug somewhere in the cockpit. "How can you go twice the speed of sound without having anywhere to place your hot or cold beverage? My Chevrolet Bel Air has a free-standing cylindrical holder; why doesn't the Arrow have one?"

> "How can you go twice the speed of sound without having anywhere to place your hot or cold beverage?" says Prime Minister John Diefenbaker

The prime minister also complained about the noise from the two Pratt & Whitney turbojets, saying that it could "wake up the dead" and that the aircraft travelled much too fast for his liking.

"Sure, it may look nice, but we'd be embarrassed in front of the Soviets or Americans if we produced such a complicated flying machine," added a dumbfounded Diefenbaker.

At press time, departing aeronautical scientists were apologizing for not reaching the standard of Canadian technological mediocrity.

## Government PSA: How to Tell at a Glance if Your Neighbour Is a Communist

*In the 1950s and 1960s, the Canadian government produced a number of PSAs to help the population locate and identify communists in their area.*

# How to Tell at a Glance if Your Neighbour Is a COMMUNIST

Communist sympathizers are everywhere. They work where you work. They shop where you shop. They might even live in your house right now. It is your patriotic duty to know what to look for and make sure the red menace stays out of Canada!

Communists think their ideology is easy, and will try to slip pro-communist sentiment into any conversation. They'll say things like "I'm a socialist, not a communist" or "I'm a member of a union," but don't be fooled. Be especially wary of those from Saskatchewan, as the province has "socialized medicine" that undermines the capitalist value of placing a price on illness and injury.

Another handy trick for spotting a "Red Peter" is to keep an eye out for anyone who behaves "weird" or "different" according to your own preconceived, subjective notions of what normal behaviour looks like. If he feels different, he's more than likely to be a communist.

Keep five feet away from any suspected communist and avoid any physical contact to prevent the spread of dangerous ideas.

Remember to report all suspicious activity to the authorities.

**PAID FOR BY THE ROYAL CANADIAN MOUNTED POLICE**

*"The refusal to carry on or participate in such work should be considered equal to treason"*

# Relocating Inuit best defence against nuclear Armageddon

*By Louis St. Laurent*

———— OCTOBER 13, 1953 ————

We call it a Cold War, as we should. Armageddon is the danger Canada faces if we are not ever-vigilant in our duty as the noble caretakers of this part of the planet. Our land, so proud, so free, and so cold 75% of the year, should be protected by those who know this country best: the Inuit.

These heroic, stoic, and patriotic souls are the best defence this country has against the marauding communist hordes from the USSR and the complete annihilation of our great nation. Our way of life, our love of democracy and justness, have no greater defenders than these people who know not the meaning of pioneer, nor trailblazer, but encapsulate both terms so beautifully. They are the real heroes our country deserves.

It is for these reasons that I have managed to convince 87 of these dignified people to move to the High Arctic. There they will not only be our citizens, they will be our human flagpoles perched at the top of the world, spears in hand, pointing the way forward in these perilous times.

They have greeted this challenge with pride, moving without hesitation to Ellesmere and Cornwallis Islands from their homes in Northern Quebec and Baffin Island. The two desolate outposts of Grise Fiord and Resolute will forever be associated with these noble acts.

> "[The Inuit] are determined to meet these challenges head on."

The 1200-kilometre journey to the edge of our land will allow these talented people to return to their roots—to be self-reliant while mastering a frozen frontier. They are not daunted by having to hunt in 24-hour darkness, by temperatures that can drop as low as −51°C, by being prevented from hunting on the wildlife preserves on nearby islands, or by being forbidden to hunt any of the muskox that are protected by international law. They are determined to meet these challenges head on, parkas facing straight into the storm.

These are hard decisions made in tough times, as only a Liberal government can do. But it's the path we must take lest we lose control of the Northwest Passage to the United States, surrender to borscht-eating, ushanka-wearing communists, or get burned beyond all recognition by nuclear fallout.

Even if all else fails, we can hold our heads high knowing that we did everything we could to send the right people into such a daunting situation.

## Toronto ferry towed by Marilyn Bell

# Police confuse "Richard Riot" with standard St. Patrick's Day in Montreal

——— MARCH 18, 1955 ———

MONTREAL — When police were called to the scene outside the Montreal Forum last night, they mistook the so-called Richard Riot as standard St. Patrick's Day debauchery.

"We pulled up outside the Forum's ticket gate and assumed the citizens had been imbibing a little too heartily," said police constable Steve McMullin, sporting two black eyes. "They wanted to get in without tickets, said something about 'Vivre Richard.' We told them to lay off the green beer and drink some water. That's when things turned sour."

Police also had troubles inside the arena.

"Normally during a game the crowd is quite respectful, being full of wealthy anglophones and all," said officer Pierre McTeague, covered with tomato stains. "I guess this year they were just a little enthusiastic. That's the luck of the Irish for you!"

Forum usher Jean-François Lemarre saw it differently. "The police had no clue what was going on," he said. "They were saying things like 'Had a little too much, have we?' and 'Need a bit of a lie down, sir?' I usually only see that when Toronto fans are in here."

The 21,000 rioters who broke windows and caused $100,000 worth of damage now make up the second most destructive St. Patrick's Day in Montreal history, trailing only the 1931 burst pipe from the Molson Brewery that precipitated a riot in the borough of Sainte-Marie.

# Diefenbaker appoints Soviet spy as minister of extramarital affairs

——— FEBRUARY 23, 1960 ———

OTTAWA — Prime Minister John Diefenbaker has welcomed a Soviet spy and East German prostitute into the federal Cabinet as the minister responsible for extramarital affairs.

Miss Gerda Munsinger was a shoo-in for the post, as she's already well briefed on the current military and security policies of Canada and of Canada's NATO allies. She's also experienced in handling private documents as well as private parts.

"Minister Munsinger will provide a much-needed service to other Cabinet ministers and high-ranking officials," explained George Hees, minister of trade and commerce. "I can't emphasize enough how well she gets along with the men. There's an energy in the room and a very hard sense of Cabinet solidarity."

Munsinger's duties include reading memorandums to Cabinet with a deep, raspy German accent, attending soirées and operas with other Cabinet ministers and high-ranking bureaucrats, and "making the boys feel real special."

Associate Minister of Defence Pierre Sévigny had nothing but praise for the woman he co-sponsored for Canadian citizenship. "I've been spending many late nights at my desk with Gerda reviewing our West German bases and the locations of our Bomarc missiles. She always brings that silly, tiny camera with her . . . but no camera could ever capture those sharp green eyes. She's copied every document with an elegance and grace that makes a man tremble and beg for more."

Despite granting a Cabinet position to a foreign national with Soviet ties, the other ministers have made sure that their activities are kept secret from the Reds, or at least their wives.

# First Nations can now vote at local residential school

——— JULY 1, 1960 ———

ST. PAUL, ALBERTA — First Nations peoples are fitting into Canada's rich tapestry more than ever now that they've been given the right to vote in federal elections at their local residential school.

Prime Minister John Diefenbaker made the announcement from Blue Quills Residential School, declaring it a great day for the queen's subjects and one they should be thankful for.

"The voices of these strong Canadians will now be heard, counted, and recounted," Diefenbaker said while wearing a mock Plains Indian headdress. "They'll be able to cast their ballot at the institution that is central to modern life for the Indian: the school their children are forced to attend."

The federal minister for the Blue Quills riding, Frank Fane, put the lasting impacts of this electoral allowance into perspective.

"As Canada continues to grow," Fane explained, "it will be important for our First Nations friends to know which of their elected representatives to complain to when we start exploiting the natural resources within their territories."

Diefenbaker ended his speech by declaring the residential school system to be a key factor in yesterday's events.

"It is a testament to Canadian education systems that they allow citizens like the First Nations to fully understand their role in how our country is run. Without this form of schooling, they wouldn't have a full grasp of the democratic process we are subjecting them to."

Diefenbaker's Alberta visit is set to continue with a relaxing dip in the Banff Hot Springs, followed by bear hunting in Jasper and concluding with a one-night stay in his Diefen-bunker in Penfold.

## Hydro-electric dams, overpasses constructed in every Quebec backyard

# Mother shamed for not permitting child to play outside unsupervised

——— JUNE 23, 1962 ———

ETOBICOKE, ON — A local woman is on the defensive after a controversial decision to supervise her seven-year-old boy while he played outside near a busy street.

Linda Jones, the mother in question and a complete worry-wart, supported her decision by citing the threat of nuclear apocalypse, widespread environmental pollution, and son Jimmy's severe pollen allergy.

Sally Tucker, a local parent, disagreed with Linda's decision.

"Far be it for me to criticize another mother's parenting, but frankly, it's terrible. If he's stuck inside, how will Jimmy ever enjoy traumatic yet enriching life lessons like finding a dead body in a ravine?"

A small but vocal group consisting of some local kids and led by Jimmy himself have vowed to oppose the decision.

"This is exactly like the time I got a set of lawn darts for my birthday but wasn't allowed to play with them," exclaimed Jimmy. "Other kids are allowed to go out and wander the streets like homeless vagrants or climb trees and break their arms. It's not fair!"

A spokesman for Child Services says that they're monitoring the situation and are prepared to intervene should they feel the child is not being exposed to sufficient "boys will be boys" levels.

# Report: EEEEEEEEEEEEEEEEEEEE!!!!!!

# Canada's best athlete a horse

TORONTO — The Lou Marsh Award, the annual honour that celebrates the best Canadian athlete from across the world of amateur and professional athletics, was given to a horse yesterday.

Northern Dancer, the fastest horse ever to win the Kentucky Derby, beat out every Canadian hockey player and Olympic athlete, not to mention all the other animals that were apparently in the running for the prize.

"It is with great honour that I accept this on Northern's behalf," said jockey Bill Hartack. "I'm sure that if Northern could speak or understand the concept of awards, he would want me to say how grateful he is."

For winning the award, the horse will get $5000, a lifetime supply of hay, and the right to bang any female horse he wants from now until his dying day.

## Within an hour of starting operation, Air Canada loses first bag

*On January 2, 1965, Trans-Canada Airlines made its inaugural commercial flight under its new name, Air Canada. Here's the heavily damaged baggage they lost on that flight from Montreal to Halifax, rediscovered in 1984.*

# Children's Canadian Flag Drawing Competition

*The Pearson government hosted a drawing competition for children aged four to nine in a bid to help it replace Canada's existing flag, the Red Ensign. Over 50,000 children across the country participated. These are the top four selected from the competition, including the winning design.*

*Elizabeth Sinclair, age 6*

*John Diefenbaker, age 69*

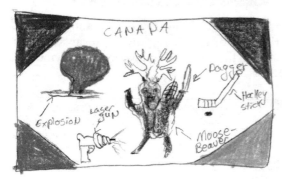

*Eddie McDonald, age 5*

*Nancy Birch, age 4*
*WINNER*

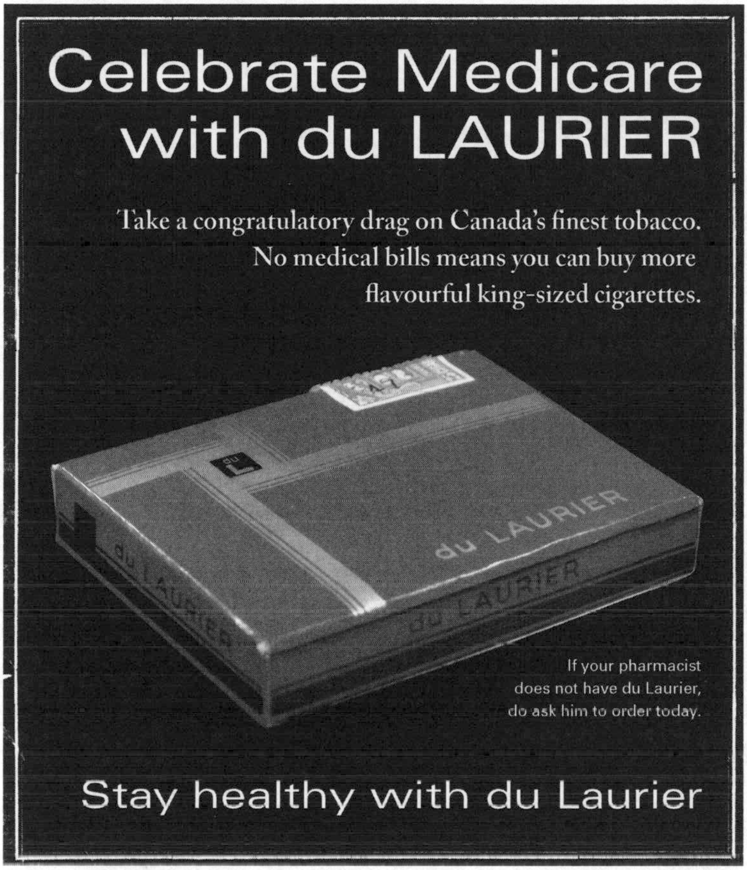

## McLuhanisms

*Herbert Marshall McLuhan was a Canadian intellectual famous for coining the phrase "The medium is the message." Here are some of his other groundbreaking philosophical tidbits.*

—

**"The tautology is the message."**

**"You just have to listen to the arguments I'm not making."**

**"The guacamole makes the avocado."**

**"I sound a lot smarter when I just turn things on their head."**

**"Pop culture philosophers can turn fifteen minutes into two hours."**

# Thousands hospitalized after celebrating passage of medicare

——— DECEMBER 19, 1966 ———

OTTAWA — Many jubilant Canadians rejoicing the passage of the Medical Care Act have injured themselves, requiring X-rays, stitches, body casts, crutches, and other forms of treatment.

The new law, which will help cover the cost of visits to the doctor outside hospitals, had encouraged some to party recklessly and take needless risks to mark the occasion.

Immediately after passage of the act, Prime Minister Lester Pearson and NDP leader Tommy Douglas gave themselves an overenthusiastic high-five, causing both of their right shoulders to dislocate.

Some Canadians stood on chairs to announce their national superiority to Americans before the chair legs gave way, resulting in sprained ankles, broken arms, and bumped heads. Clumsy revellers from St. John's to Victoria tripped and stumbled over each other in the large crowds that formed at city halls across the nation. An impromptu fireworks demonstration in Miramichi, New Brunswick, has burned several, and a man lost three fingers after lighting a short fuse. In Canada's Territories, eight suffered from frostbite as they gathered outside in −42°C weather to cheer and sing "O Canada."

The patients' upbeat mood soon soured when physicians informed them that they still had to pay for their prescription painkillers, home care, and medical devices when they left hospital or the doctor's office. Making matters worse, the Medical Care Act will not come into effect until July 1, 1968.

# THE BEAVERTON

WEDNESDAY, MAY 3, 1967

70 PAGES
unless we mis-counted

50 CENTS
at newsstand

**MORNING** edition

# Hockey experts predict Leafs will win 20 more Cups before year 2000

By EDGAR TOFT
Beaverton Staff Reporter

TORONTO—With the Maple Leafs coming off a run of four Stanley Cups in six years, hockey experts are already predicting the team will win 20 or more championships before the end of the 20th century.

The Leafs defeated the Montreal Canadiens last night four games to two to win their 13th title. Analysts are now certain that there's no stopping the Toronto club.

"Many dismissed this team as being too old and too slow, but they still pack a punch and have plenty of experienced, talented players," said NHL expert Lou Beirtwart. "The fact of the matter is, when you're a team as well-run and well-respected as the Maple Leafs, success is sure to follow."

Analysts say that Leafs management will make smart choices in trades and contracts in order to maintain an outstanding roster of players, especially when it comes to goaltending.

The expansion of the league should pose no problem for the indefatigable team, which features some of the best hockey players in their mid-40s—including Johnny Bower, who made 400 saves with his face in the 66-67 season.

In related news, the City of Toronto has announced that it will widen Yonge Street and add permanent bleachers in order to accommodate all future Stanley Cup parades.

## Keon uses Cup as

# Mid-Life
# CRISIS
## (1967–1999)

"Masters in our own house we must be, but our house is the whole of Canada. So get out of our house, Your Majesty." —Pierre Trudeau

As the country turned 100, Canada had to find a new identity (again). We had to be more than just America's cousin or Britain's distant child who never calls anymore. Pierre Trudeau's entry on the scene made Canada a sexy place to be for the first time since Wilfrid Laurier's famous nip slip. In Quebec, the Quiet Revolution gave way to the separatist movement, two referendums, and smoked meat sandwiches. The West got angry, B.C. got really high, and the Maritimes experienced a few hours of uninterrupted economic prosperity.

# KEY DATES

**June 15, 1968**
Prime Minister Pierre Trudeau pantses
Opposition leader Robert Stanfield
during first televised election debate

**March 12, 1970**
Peacekeepers deployed to
Canada to quell metric system
conversion–related violence

**November 1, 1971**
Canada's first major fake newspaper,
the *Toronto Sun*, begins publication

**September 17, 1974**
RCMP woos first female officers
with recruitment catcalls,
unwanted invitations for drinks
to talk about policing

**October 3, 1981**
Trivial Pursuit gives Canadians
new board game to fight about

**February 3, 1985**
Prime Minister Brian Mulroney and
President Ronald Reagan kiss for
the first time on live television

**January 1, 1991**
Millions of generous Canadians volunteer
to pay GST to help government out
until it can get back on its feet

**July 12, 1994**
Alice Munro's angry Letter to the
Editor about no-good youth in a
fading small Ontario town wins
Governor General's Award

**May 2, 1998**
Canadian dollar, Mexican
peso reach parity

# Voyeuristic bureaucrats no longer allowed in the bedrooms of the nation

———— DECEMBER 22, 1967 ————

OTTAWA — Despite the prospect of leaving many civil servants unsatisfied, Justice Minister Pierre Trudeau has announced that the government will be closing the Department of Morality offices currently located in every single bedroom across the country.

"The government of Canada will not spy on our citizens," said Trudeau at a press conference. "We will no longer use live cameras, fantasy sketches, or play-by-play narration of Canadians' most intimate, private moments in order to ensure that no one is gay."

Following the announcement, "curious" government workers began emptying their desks and nightstands and clearing their filing cabinets of reports on the sexual preferences of all 20 million Canadians. These reports are alleged to contain explicit photos as well as detailed information on citizens' favourite positions and preferred types of intercourse.

In addition, Trudeau ordered the immediate halt to the Public Service's "Watch and Stare" policy, which requires any public servant to stand outside homes' open windows if they suspect sexual activity will occur.

"The state has no place in the bedrooms of the nation," said Trudeau to the press. "Unless you're into that. In which case we may be able to work something out."

# Bilingualism achieved after customs official learns "bonjour"

———— NOVEMBER 17, 1969 ————

CALGARY — Demonstrating the success of the Official Languages Act, customs official Arnold Griech greeted passengers in both official languages at Calgary's international airport yesterday.

The term *bonjour* is the French word for "hello" or "good day" and was used interchangeably by Griech before he switched to English to ask why passengers were visiting Canada.

Mastering the seven letter word, and therefore the French language, didn't come easily for the federal official. The 47-year-old anglophone has worked in English for over two decades, but was required to take an eight-week intensive course on the French greeting to obtain his official bilingual status.

## Africville demolished to make way for new multicultural centre

——— JANUARY 3, 1970 ———

HALIFAX — The black neighbourhood of Africville outside Halifax has been completely destroyed in order to clear the site for construction of the new Canadian Multicultural Centre.

The last shred of black Canadian history in the area was levelled late last night when bulldozers brought down the sole remaining house that paid property taxes but never received any city services. Unlike these former structures, the 400,000-square-foot museum will receive such amenities as water, electricity, and legal rights.

"The $2 million facility will be a great way to celebrate diversity on this previously occupied land," explained Halifax mayor Allan O'Brien. "We're no longer going to sweep this area under the rug because we used it as a city landfill. It will now become a place where all Canadians can come together and feel great about themselves for having such a diverse country."

The educational facility will showcase the contributions of Polish, Ukrainian, Polish-Ukrainian, Irish, the different type of Irish, British, English, Scottish, Welsh, French, and "Other" Canadians.

"I can assure you that we'll have at least one African-Caribbean-Multi-Asian Canadian exhibit somewhere in the basement area," said Doug McClintock, the Centre's curator. "According to the layout of our facility, the Native Canadian exhibit will be placed immediately on top of the former graveyard, and the races-holding-hands 'Happy Friendship Circle' scene will rest on the former school playground."

Sources inside the Centre say the facility will also feature a kids' game that will hyphenate their identity according to their race and genealogy.

## FLQ cell needs Bescherelle to write this week's ransom note

——— OCTOBER 20, 1970 ———

MONTREAL — Members of the Front de libération du Québec's "Liberation Cell" were forced to use a Bescherelle after struggling with French grammar in their weekly ransom note.

"Is the sentence 'Any further military escalation will result in the immediate execution of James Cross' in futur antérieur or futur simple?" asked one kidnapper of another while skimming through a verb conjugation guide.

"Beats me," replied the second kidnapper, who held a gun up to the British trade commissioner's head. "I never learned that stuff. Did you check the back?"

The kidnappers began to argue about which relative pronoun to use while declaring their violent revolution against the Canadian state and their plans for Quebec's future as an independent socialist utopia.

"Don't forget to call Trudeau a queer!" reminded a third kidnapper, who was watching the news on the mass arrests occurring in Montreal.

According to sources, the cell was planning on mailing the ransom letter to the authorities, but realized that most of the surrounding mailboxes had already been blown up by other FLQ members.

## PM orders invasion of Quebec

***Navy deployed to St. Lawrence to deter FLQ's nuclear submarines***

——— OCTOBER 21, 1970 ———

MONTREAL — Tanks, helicopters, and over 10,000 Canadian soldiers have crossed the Ottawa River into Quebec to reassert the control it already has over the population.

While the Quebec government made the request for military assistance to aid civil power, the Liberal government is taking no chances and has launched a full-scale assault on Montreal and Quebec City.

All symbols of Canada in Quebec—from statues to government offices—have been heavily fortified with barbed wire, sandbags, and landmines. Inflatable Canada Post mailbox decoys have also been deployed along streets of Montreal in an effort to bait any possible radical revolutionaries.

CF-104s flying combat air patrols roared over the skies of Quebec, but have yet to intercept any militant Quebec separatist MiGs.

"Anyone uttering a word of French will be thrown into jail without charge, and that includes me," decreed Trudeau from the top of a Centurion Tank parked at a Montreal elementary school. "We have to presume that anyone could be the enemy and, therefore, is the enemy."

## Trudeau: "I didn't say 'fuddle duddle'; I said 'fuck off'"

——— FEBRUARY 16, 1971 ———

OTTAWA — Clarifying his remarks to an Opposition MP in the House of Commons, Prime Minister Pierre Trudeau insisted that he'd said "Fuck off, you stupid piece of shit" instead of "Fuddle duddle."

The incident occurred when Progressive Conservative MP Lincoln Alexander asked the Liberal government what it was doing about the nation's unemployed and the prime minister could be seen mouthing the words in response.

Fellow Tory MP John Lundrigan rose on a point of order. "Mr. Speaker, please excuse the unparliamentary language, but did the prime minister just direct the 'FD' words at the member for Hamilton West?"

When the Speaker reminded parliamentarians to keep their off-colour remarks to profanities instead of nonsensical terms, the prime minister shook his head.

The media pressed Trudeau on his use of the term. "What I clearly said was 'Fuck off,' and I can't make that any clearer. The term I've been accused of using is not at all what I said, for that would be incredibly childish, and anyone who tells you I said it is a gaping asshole full of shit. Now if you'll excuse me I have some real fucking work to do."

## Feminist bride smashes patriarchy by keeping father's last name

——— MARCH 28, 1972 ———

OSHAWA, ON — Feminist Laura Wilson has made a radical step toward equality by keeping her father's last name rather than changing it when she gets married next week.

"The patriarchy says that women should be the property of our husbands," said Wilson, "but I intend to keep my own identity as the property of my father."

Wilson's dad, Larry, was proud of his offspring for keeping the family name despite his having been unable to produce a son.

"Four daughters . . . four of them," said Larry, staring forlornly into an empty scotch glass. "I guess it's some consolation that her last name won't be Kilgore, but I'm iffy on the Wilson-Kilgore name for the grandchildren. I mean, won't that confuse them in their early years and make them queer?"

According to sources inside the wedding party, Wilson will not be wearing the traditional white, but will still pay three paycheques' worth for the one-time-use dress.

# Soviet Newspaper: '72 Summit Series

## МЕДВЕДЬ
### THE BEAR
*"The Soviet Union's English Newspaper"*

ТЫ ЧЁ EDITION     SEPTEMBER 29, 1972     60 CENTS

## GLORIOUS SOVIET TEAM DEFEATS CANADIANS IN SUMMIT SERIES
### MOTHERLAND WINS ALL 8 GAMES IN SHUTOUTS

MOSCOW — Showing the strength of the mighty Soviet Union, our hockey team easily defeated the lesser Canadian squad in the 1972 Summit Series. The final game's score was 30–0 for the Soviets, who overwhelmed their opponents with superior plays, organization, and economic system.

Alexander Yakushev, who scored over 100 goals in the tournament, thanked the pre-eminence of Soviet training and its Five-Year Ice Hockey Plan. "Long live Secretary Brezhnev and the Communist party for allowing the puck to glide into the Canadian net! Soviet hockey, unite!"

Canadian forward Phil Esposito, who reportedly cried through most of the tournament, was also said to cower when confronting our towering forwards. Paul Henderson reportedly peed his hockey trousers every time he came near the puck for fear of confronting a liberated proletariat on skates.

Our goaltender stopped every shot the Canadians could muster with consummate grace and ease.

The Soviet victory is yet another illustration of the supremacy of the communist hockey system and the evils of capitalist Canada and other Western countries.

Poll: 100% of Poland believes communism best for country, p. 4

East German Trabant cars: The most reliable auto made from compressed cardboard, p. 8

**THE FOLLOWING PEOPLE ARE SPIES FOR THE WEST**
- **Foster Hewitt**
- **Harry Sinden**

---

# Football Robert Stanfield fumbled appointed to Senate

*'Pigskin played an instrumental role in Liberal electoral victory,' says Trudeau*

JULY 10, 1974

OTTAWA — The football that foiled any chance of Progressive Conservative leader Robert Stanfield's becoming prime minister has been rewarded with an appointment to the Senate.

Prime Minister Pierre Trudeau made the announcement a day after winning a convincing majority government, in large part owing to the leather-bound ball's ability to avoid the grasp of the Opposition leader that one time it was thrown to him.

"This Spalding football worked hard throughout its life, and it answered the call when

we needed it most," Trudeau said of his newest patronage appointment. "I couldn't ask any more of a supporter."

The football's ability to demonstrate Stanfield's momentary clumsiness and emasculation struck a chord with voters. Any of his convincing arguments about job creation or controlling inflation went out the window once Stanfield had illustrated his unfitness as a wide receiver and therefore as a prime minister.

According to sources, the football is the most qualified and vocal senator to ever be appointed in Canadian history.

# Joe Clark becomes youngest prime minister by using fake ID

———— JUNE 4, 1979 ————

OTTAWA — Joe Clark has become the youngest person ever to obtain the title of prime minister after using a very real-looking driver's licence that indicated he was much older than he actually is.

The 39-year-old MP for the Yellowhead riding had been using the false document for several years so that he could be declared a candidate for MP, win the PC leadership convention, and impress several of his friends.

"Are you sure you're 61?" asked Governor General Edward Schreyer at the swearing-in ceremony as he compared the photo on the Alberta driver's licence to Clark's face.

"Yes, that is a 100% legal, authentic licence," said Clark, whose voice sounded nervous and cracked.

The governor general quizzed the youngster about details on the ID, including whether his real middle name was actually Wilbur.

"It says your eyes are brown, but they're quite blue when I look at you," said a perplexed Schreyer. "And on the back of the licence, it says it expired in 1977."

Clark, who'd begun to visibly perspire, responded that it was just an error and that he hadn't the time to visit the provincial Motor Vehicle Branch recently to make the change.

After the ceremony declaring Clark to be the country's 16th prime minister, he gave high-fives to all his friends before leaving Rideau Hall in a pickup truck to drink rye whisky along the Ottawa River.

# MONTREAL OLYMPIC STADIUM

*Water-soluble concrete pillars*

*Condom-like stadium design to remind everyone about safe sex*

*Several secret meeting locations where the contractors and union bosses can be paid their proper kickbacks*

*Collapsible roof*

*Giant scoreboard for counting stadium's accumulating debt*

## René Lévesque smokes 43 cigarettes for sovereignty

# Terry Fox backtracks 2000 kms after forgetting to lock front door

———— JUNE 28, 1980 ————

HAWKESBURY, ON — The young man who has inspired millions of Canadians in his effort to raise awareness and money for cancer by running across the country suddenly realized that he forgot to lock the front door of an apartment he was staying at in St. John's, Newfoundland.

"Oh shit!" exclaimed Fox to himself as he approached a cheering crowd of supporters and well-wishers. "No, I definitely forgot. We have to go back. I'm sorry, everyone."

Fox immediately began running back east, planning to make up the time by running two marathons every day for the rest of the trip.

"It's so annoying, but if I don't go back I'm going to be thinking about it for the entire Marathon of Hope. Also, I just realized how much easier it is to run with the wind at your back instead of at your face."

When Fox arrived at the apartment, he discovered that he had in fact locked the door. But he had a sneaking suspicion that he'd left the oven on at one of the places he stayed in Quebec.

## Canadian Voices: Terry Fox

Terry Fox, a young man whose leg was amputated due to cancer, is running across Canada—from St. John's, Newfoundland, to Victoria, B.C.—to raise money for cancer research, making him a national hero. What's your say?

"He'd get there a lot quicker if he drove."
CHAD TROST, REGINA

"I once walked to school in January with no gloves."
ETHYL CARPENTER, SURREY

"I've been really inspired to amputate my own leg."
MORRIS DAVID, MONTREAL

## Trudeau instructs Canadarm to extend middle finger every time it orbits over Alberta

———— NOVEMBER 12, 1981 ————

143 KM ABOVE THE EARTH — In a move that has further escalated tension between the prime minister and the West, Pierre Trudeau has ordered that NASA extend the robotic Canadarm's middle finger every time it orbits over the province of Alberta.

Canadarm's Bird 1 on board the Columbia Space Shuttle was fully extended for the first time by U.S. and British astronauts during the 21.3 seconds it passed over the Prairie province.

"This move is a symbolic message to Albertans about who really controls natural resources," said the prime minister. "Also, I wanted to let all Albertans know that they can go fuck themselves."

Observing from a powerful telescope, Alberta premier Peter Lougheed muttered to himself "That son of a bitch" before instructing provincial officials to cut oil production again.

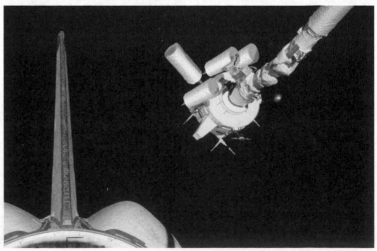

# Gay Bathhouse Raids:
# Search Warrant

## WARRANT TO SEARCH
PURSUANT TO SECTION ▓▓▓▓ OF THE *CANADIAN CRIMINAL CODE*

OPERATION SOAP

**CANADA**
**PROVINCE OF ONTARIO**

**TORONTO REGION**

To the Peace Officers in the Province of Ontario or to the:

_____
*(Named Public Officers)*

WHEREAS it appears on the oath of _____ CONSTABLE BRUCE "SLENDERLEGS" JOHNSON _____

a Peace Officer in Metropolitan Toronto, in the Province of Ontario, THAT there are reasonable grounds for

believing that the following offences have been committed: *(describe offences, etc.)*

BEING TOTALLY GAY OF THE HIGHEST ORDER, CONTRARY TO GOD
AND ALL THINGS HOLY, AND SOME SECTION SOMEWHERE OF THE
CRIMINAL CODE

ASSAULTING A POLICEMAN'S BRITTLE SENSE OF MASCULINITY
WITH GAYNESS

AND THAT there are reasonable grounds for believing that the following items will afford evidence of the offences:

*(describe offences, etc.)*

BREAKING ALL THE WALLS OF THE ESTABLISHMENT;

LOTS OF SWEATY GAY MEN DOING GAY THINGS TO EACH OTHER GAYLY.

AND THAT there are reasonable grounds for believing that said items or some part of them are in: *(describe place to search)*

THE CLUB BATHS, TORONTO, ON;

THE ROMANS II HEALTH AND RECREATION SPA, TORONTO, ON;

THE RICHMOND STREET HEALTH EMPORIUM, TORONTO, ON;

THE BARRACKS, TORONTO, ON. ("THE PREMISES")

THIS IS THEREFORE to authorize and require that you enter said premises between the hours of __11:00 P.M.__

on __FEB. 5, 1981__ , and __8:00 A.M.__ on __FEB. 6, 1981__ , to search for the things and bring them before

me or some other Justice, or submit a report in writing with respect to any of the gay shit you find.

DATE this __5TH__ day of __FEBRUARY__ , __1981__ , at Toronto, in the Province of Ontario.

_____
ROY MCMURTRY
Attorney General of Ontario

## Mrs. Oakley's Grade 6 Language Arts Reading of *The Hockey Sweater*

—

### GOAL:

Ensure that students read about and understand the important lessons of the story *The Hockey Sweater*.

### OVERVIEW:

*The Hockey Sweater*, a childhood recollection by Roch Carrier, is a classic Canadian book about the game of hockey, Quebec society, and growing up in Quebec during the era of the iconic Maurice Richard.

### KEY POINTS OF THE BOOK:

• Don't be different or else your friends and religious leaders will mistreat you.

• If you are different, it's your mother's fault.

• If a popular hockey player does something, you do it too.

• Ravenous moths may one day destroy your unwanted clothes if you pray hard enough.

• Leafs suck.

### EXERCISE:

Have all but one of the students wear red sweaters. The lone student will wear blue. Ensure that he is mistreated for the rest of the day for further emphasis.

# Queen Elizabeth steals pen after signing new Canadian Constitution

——— APRIL 17, 1982 ———

OTTAWA — Queen Elizabeth stealthily acquired a new pen after signing the Constitution Act, thereby causing a massive delay in repatriating the Constitution.

After Canada's head of state so gracefully pocketed the fountain pen without anyone noticing, Prime Minister Pierre Trudeau was seen checking his pockets to see whether he had a spare.

"Your Highness, do you have that pen you just used?" asked the PM.

The queen replied by shaking her head. "What pen? I didn't see any pen. I only see a Constitution Act with my signature already on it."

An annoyed Trudeau looked at his ministers, who shrugged. The triumphant music stopped abruptly. The prime minister was forced to stand up from his chair and yell, "Does anyone have a pen?"

"I've got one!" exclaimed Justice Minister Jean Chrétien, to the relief of the crowd. However, after Trudeau's several attempts to get the ink running by scribbling on the Constitution, the pen proved useless. Bureaucrats scrambled to look in every drawer in Ottawa to see whether someone, somewhere had a functioning writing implement so that the ceremony could proceed.

"We've found countless rubber bands and paper clips, but no pens," explained Governor General Edward Schreyer. "We did find a pencil, however. Would that work?"

"I can't use a pencil. What if someone erases it?" replied Trudeau, rebuking the queen's representative.

At press time, the queen was overheard saying, "That'll teach the peasant king not to pirouette behind me ever again."

# Flash in the Pan: John Turner's Reflections as Prime Minister

*Although John Turner had a long career in federal politics, he served as prime minister for only about 37 seconds. Here's an excerpt from his three-paragraph memoir of his experience.*

——— JULY 23, 1984 ———

"Rideau Hall was a bit stuffy that day, so I had to loosen my collar. The swearing-in ceremony was very emotional for me. I remember the immense feeling of pride and satisfaction, but I was also very humbled to serve the people of Canada. I had a plan to create jobs and to make Canada a player on the global stage.

I had this odd sensation when my chief of staff addressed me for the first time as "Mr. Prime Minister" before adding "you just lost the election to Brian Mulroney."

## Rick Hansen makes his way up CN Tower

# Brian Mulroney appears on *Degrassi Junior High* to promote Meech Lake Accord

———— OCTOBER 17, 1987 ————

TORONTO — Prime Minister Brian Mulroney has made a special guest appearance on the popular CBC television show *Degrassi Junior High*, playing a grade 9 student named Sid who's worried that his classmates don't understand the need for Quebec to sign the repatriated Constitution.

During his two-episode storyline, Sid can be seen explaining why the Accord will help keep Canada united, and then trying marijuana for the first time.

"Good morning, fellow students," Sid says, wearing a sweater tied around his polo shirt. "I'd like to talk to you about an impor tant issue affecting the entire school and the nation: recognizing Quebec as a distinct society. This constitutional amendment is a significant symbolic gesture.

We should do our part in supporting the prime minister's initiative in this critical agreement on our federation.

"Also, the Zit Remedy rocks so hard!"

Sid then makes an agreement with Stephanie, the student president, whereby she'll put up pro–Meech Lake posters in the cafeteria as long as he goes to the school dance with her to make Wheels feel jealous.

However, plans to persuade the young people backfire when many accuse Sid of being a smooth-talker and trying to get a date with Caitlin while Joey tries to use a fake ID to get into a strip club.

At the end of the episode, Miles, an ardent opponent of Meech Lake because of its lack of public consultation, burns down Sid's poster and, subsequently, the entire school.

## 1988 Free Trade Debate: Quotes

—

*"Free trade will give Canada a trade surplus in manu-facturing jobs exported to the U.S., making Canada a leader in something."*
**PRIME MINISTER BRIAN MULRONEY**

*"We will start digging a trench along the 49th parallel for the inevitable U.S. invasion of Canada; Canadians should ready their muskets."*
**OFFICIAL OPPOSITION LEADER JOHN TURNER**

*"I will tattoo a Maple Leaf on my face if I win this election. I am totally fucking serious. I'll do it."*
**NDP LEADER ED BROADBENT**

# Coat hanger industry decries Morgentaler's Supreme Court victory

OTTAWA — The coat hanger lobby is warning that its entire industry could collapse now that the law prohibiting abortion has been deemed to violate the Charter of Rights and Freedoms.

McIver and Sons Metal Coat Hangers Ltd., an intervener in the Supreme Court case, argued unsuccessfully that decriminalizing abortion services will severely weaken the demand for wire coat hooks and lead to widespread unemployment.

"This is a sad day for the thousands of workers at our plants across the country," said CEO Marv Christie, whose company had just announced layoffs at factories in Melville, Chatham, Trois-Rivières, and Appleton. "Without the business we get from terrified teenage girls trying to keep their pregnancy a secret and exhausted mothers of four or more children who can't afford to have another, we won't be able to continue to operate."

The Gin and Hot Bath lobby, the Knitting Needles Association, and the Epsom Salts union had all joined in the ultimately futile effort to criminalize abortion and demonize Dr. Henry Morgentaler throughout the long legal battle.

"This is clearly a miscarriage of justice for us all," added Christie.

# Ben Johnson loses gold after testing positive for more performance-enhancing drugs than competitors

SEOUL — Canadian sprinter Ben Johnson has been stripped of the 100-metre gold medal after IOC officials discovered that the athlete had more steroids and stimulants in his body than his competitors did.

In a statement, the IOC said that Johnson will have his 9.79-second world record rescinded, since the amount of stanozolol in his blood represented "an unreasonable amount of cheating."

"He's really ruining it for the rest of us," said Johnson's American competitor Carl Lewis, who tested positive for the stimulants pseudoephedrine, ephedrine, and phenylpropanolamine during the Olympic trials. "You can't consume that stuff 'accidentally' like I did and get away with it."

British sprinter Dennis Mitchell, who was bumped up to silver after Johnson's disqualification, said that, like everyone else in the field, he takes a reasonable amount of pseudoephedrine to enhance his performance but nothing like the excess of Johnson's use.

"It has to be competitive," said Mitchell, who had a questionable amount of a banned substance in his blood after he ran the 200-metre heats. "Otherwise, they might ban performance-enhancing drugs entirely, making the sport no fun to watch."

In related news, the Bulgarian weightlifting team has set a new world record in the amount of banned substances in an athlete's blood.

## Reagan puts Canada–U.S. Free Trade Agreement in fridge again

——— JANUARY 13, 1988 ———

WASHINGTON, D.C. — U.S. president Ronald Reagan has stashed the Canada–U.S. Free Trade Agreement in the White House kitchen's refrigerator for the second time in as many weeks.

Rather than delivering the agreement to Congress for fast-track ratification, the president unwittingly misplaced the document that outlines the removal of tariffs on trade between the two countries.

"Do you remember your friend Brian?" asked Secretary of State George P. Schultz very loudly and clearly so the 40th president of the United States could understand that he was still pals with Prime Minister Brian Mulroney. "Your friend Brian and you signed this nice international agreement."

"Who are you!?" exclaimed a surprised president before remembering that Schultz was a member of his Cabinet. "Oh . . . oh . . . yes. My friend Brian. I remember Brian, yes, that nice lad from Nebraska. We sang together in Hollywood and rode bikes along the Mississippi. He once caught a redfish as big as my arm and owned a donkey. Is it Christmas yet?"

After being reminded for the second time to submit the trade deal to Congress, Reagan placed the 146-page document in the presidential pantry beside his car keys.

However, Reagan's advisers were unconcerned about the

president's forgetfulness, as half the U.S. population was unaware of the agreement in the first place.

# If only the Mohawks knew how to play golf, the Oka Crisis wouldn't have happened

*By Rt. Hon. Brian Mulroney*

——— SEPTEMBER 27, 1990 ———

I'm sure many of you were horrified to see the events unfold in Oka, Quebec, earlier this year when Mohawk terrorists seized a planned golf course—what they call "traditional land"—from the Town of Oka. But after all the violence and military mobilization, I realized that this confrontation could have been avoided if only the Mohawk people had been taught how to play golf on their ancestral grounds.

When the town began planning to expand its stunning private golf club, the mayor, with whom I've played several rounds, decided to provide a gift to the Mohawks by beautifying their territory and turning it into a profitable business. But we were not aware that the Mohawks did not play, nor had any interest in, the sport.

After years of colonization and land appropriation, the government had failed to teach the Mohawks and many other Native groups how to enjoy a sport that involves 18 holes and requires lots of land and hitting a small white ball.

This incident should be a wake-up call about the poor golf education on reserves and the lack of available facilities and equipment. We must do more to promote cross-cultural golfing initiatives and teach Aboriginal bands how to give up their land for golfing enjoyment. That way, Indigenous people would have a better understanding of why their land is being developed without their consent.

Together, we can hit the links.

# Alanis Morissette's Grade 12 English
# Exam on the Definition of Irony

Teacher: Ms. Wendelclerk

Name: _Alanis Morissette_ ENG3

### ENGLISH AND LITERATURE 1201:
### POP QUIZ

1. Describe some examples of *dramatic irony*:

Rain on a wedding day, good advice you just didn't take

*No — rain on a wedding day happens quite often and not taking advice is not a form of irony.*

2. Describe some examples of *verbal irony*:

Having too many spoons when you need a knife, meeting the man of your dreams when he is already married

*No, not quite.*

3. Describe some examples of *situational irony*:

A free ride when you've already paid, winning the lottery and dying the next day

*These are just unfortunate events, Alanis.*

*Total grade: 0/3*

*If you spent less time playing music and more time studying, you would have had a higher grade.*

# New prime minister to be paid 30% less in salary

——————— JUNE 25, 1993 ———————

OTTAWA — Canada's first female prime minister, Kim Campbell, will cost taxpayers 30% less than regular prime ministers.

Members of the Progressive Conservative party have informed Campbell that her $163,000 salary will be reduced to $114,000, since "domestic prime ministerial duties are expected of them anyway." There was also concern that the 46-year-old "will probably get pregnant and need to take a year off."

"Greeting foreign dignitaries and addressing the House of Commons during Question Period involve talking and not much else," said Treasury Board President Jim Edwards, who reviewed the prime minister's work plan after Brian Mulroney's retirement. "Plus, we've determined that making decisions about key legislation and representing Canada on a global stage are now considered administrative tasks."

Campbell has also been given more unpaid duties, including minding the young children of Cabinet ministers. In addition, there were some concerns that the woman who served as Canada's first female justice minister and its first defence minister would need a male Cabinet minister around to guide her through the complicated world of diplomacy, the military, finance, and Canadian law.

In response to Campbell's historic achievement for women, an all-male Canadian CEO panel declared that sexism was a thing of the past.

## UN Paperwork Required for Intervening in an Ongoing Massacre

*Thousands of Canadian Forces members have served in UN-mandated peacekeeping missions around the world. Here's an excerpt from just some of the paperwork a platoon had to fill out before intervening in the ongoing massacre in Bosnia.*

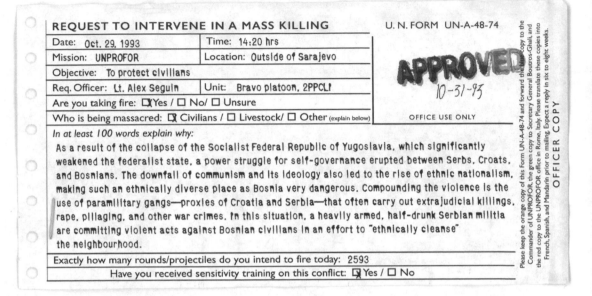

**REQUEST TO INTERVENE IN A MASS KILLING**

U. N. FORM UN-A-48-74

| | |
|---|---|
| Date: Oct. 29, 1993 | Time: 14:20 hrs |
| Mission: UNPROFOR | Location: Outside of Sarajevo |
| Objective: To protect civilians | |
| Req. Officer: Lt. Alex Seguin | Unit: Bravo platoon, 2PPCLI |

Are you taking fire: ☒ Yes / ☐ No/ ☐ Unsure

Who is being massacred: ☒ Civilians / ☐ Livestock/ ☐ Other (explain below)

**APPROVED**
10-31-93

OFFICE USE ONLY

*In at least 100 words explain why:*

As a result of the collapse of the Socialist Federal Republic of Yugoslavia, which significantly weakened the federalist state, a power struggle for self-governance erupted between Serbs, Croats, and Bosnians. The downfall of communism and its ideology also led to the rise of ethnic nationalism, making such an ethnically diverse place as Bosnia very dangerous. Compounding the violence is the use of paramilitary gangs—proxies of Croatia and Serbia—that often carry out extrajudicial killings, rape, pillaging, and other war crimes. In this situation, a heavily armed, half-drunk Serbian militia are committing violent acts against Bosnian civilians in an effort to "ethnically cleanse" the neighbourhood.

Exactly how many rounds/projectiles do you intend to fire today: 2593

Have you received sensitivity training on this conflict: ☒ Yes / ☐ No

Please keep the orange copy of this Form UN-A-48-74 and forward the blue copy to the Commander copy of UNPROFOR, the green copy to Secretary General Boutros-Ghali, and the red copy to the UNPROFOR office in Rome, Italy. Please translate these copies into French, Spanish, and Mandarin prior to mailing. Expect a reply in six to eight weeks.

OFFICER COPY

---

# Brian Tobin lands 10,000-ton Spanish fishing trawler

———— MARCH 10, 1995 ————

ST. JOHN'S — In a press conference earlier today, federal Fisheries and Oceans Minister Brian Tobin announced that he'd caught and landed a large Spanish trawler that had been fishing off the Grand Banks.

"We didn't catch anything the previous day, but as luck would have it, I got a bite," stated a triumphant Tobin as he posed next to the trawler. "Before I lost her, I set the hook. I was on a wild ride morning and afternoon. She put up a good fight and nearly snapped my line."

The record-breaking 10,000-ton catch attracted local media attention. As a reward, Tobin earned a free meal at Chee's Fish and Chips restaurant and a $500,000 bond from the owners of the vessel.

Later that evening, Tobin bragged to his friends at a bar that the trawler was "thiiiiiiis big," extending both his arms to illustrate the size.

In accordance with federal regulations, the Spanish crew was released back into the ocean so that they may return to their native waters off the European coast to spawn new trawlers.

# Gigantic Canadian flag suffocates dozens at Unity Rally

——— OCTOBER 28, 1995 ———

MONTREAL — The death toll is still rising after a gigantic Canadian flag suffocated many No supporters at the so-called Unity Rally four days ago.

The 165-square-metre Maple Leaf flag was unravelled in an effort to show support for federalism in Quebec, but the immense size of the rectangular banner was simply too much for the assembled volunteers to handle.

Cries for more oxygen from those trapped beneath the flag were muted by the loud singing of "O Canada" by proud Canadians in a show of solidarity with Quebec.

Despite the No side's narrow victory in the referendum, the monstrous fabric symbol of Canadian pride continues to terrorize Montreal, threatening to consume all citizens in its path.

# "I meant to say 'the Jews,'" clarifies Parizeau after controversial referendum concession speech

——— OCTOBER 31, 1995 ———

QUEBEC CITY — Quebec premier Jacques Parizeau has apologized for his remarks blaming "money and the ethnic vote" for the defeat of the Yes side in the Quebec referendum and has said that from now on he will simply call them "Jews."

As Parizeau explained to the press, "My statement was unfortunately misconstrued as possibly being about multiple different ethnic groups. To be clear, I was referring to those crafty Hebes who live in Outremont and stole our sovereignty."

The politician who spent years trying to establish an independent Quebec said he'd had a little too much to drink before making the speech and accidentally took his anger out on many groups of people rather than the one he truly blamed.

"I would like to apologize to the Greek, Italian, Haitian, Chinese, Irish, Portuguese, and Lebanese communities, as well as every other group who did not kill Christ. I thought that when I linked 'money' and 'ethnic vote,' everyone would know who I was talking about. I should have chosen more appropriate words, such as 'the leaders of the global financial cabal who seek world domination.'"

Parizeau added that Quebec will one day become a sovereign country after the people learn which ethnic group is responsible for dividing them.

# Tie Domi, Rob Ray jaw at each other on ice over French existentialist philosophy

———— FEBRUARY 8, 1996 ————

TORONTO — Two NHL enforcers got into a heated exchange at Maple Leaf Gardens last night over their different views of French existential philosophy.

Given their history, it didn't take long before Tie Domi of the Toronto Maple Leafs and Rob Ray of the Buffalo Sabres starting throwing verbal punches at each other for their opinions on human authenticity. Toronto's leading philosophical scrapper started chirping Buffalo's absurdism brawler before levelling Ray with a late Marxist revolutionary hit, for which Domi received a penalty.

Ray wouldn't tolerate Domi's high elbow jab, let alone his mockery of Albert Camus's view that the ends do not necessarily justify the means, and immediately dropped the gloves when Domi left the penalty box.

After they duked it out on the ice, where fists and several references to the German phenomenological movement were exchanged, referees managed to separate the pair. But the feud didn't end there; more words were exchanged on Maurice Merleau-Ponty's views of consciousness and perception.

"You're really into the Russian guys now, aren't you?" Ray said, referring to Domi's recent writings based on an existentialist interpretation of the fall of the Soviet Union. "Don't you understand that violence against innocents, like that cheap shot against my rookie tonight, delegitimizes any cause?"

"Sartre rejected authoritarian tendencies, asshole!" retorted Domi. "Morality is based on selected reality. Your arguments seem to disappear as easily as your jersey. Stay the hell out of the academy and the crease."

After the match, *Hockey Night in Canada* host Don Cherry claimed that these existentialist fights are all part of the game.

# RCMP bodyguards tackle Chrétien after he strangles several protesters

———— FEBRUARY 16, 1996 ————

OTTAWA — RCMP bodyguards tackled Prime Minister Jean Chrétien after he assaulted several protesters, tourists, and bystanders who were gathered around Parliament Hill yesterday.

The incident occurred just after the prime minister arrived at the House of Commons. Sources say Chrétien was allowed to get too close to the protests and began strangling several demonstrators who were there for different causes.

RCMP officers attempted to stop Chrétien, but the Little Guy from Shawinigan proved to be too quick for them.

> "I was so excited to see the prime minister, especially on Flag Day," explained a tourist from Prince Albert, Saskatchewan

"I was just standing here when the prime minister approached me and went straight for my neck," said Greenpeace's Greg Hilton, who'd been protesting the Japanese whale hunt.

Other victims appeared to have no particular agenda.

"I was so excited to see the prime minister, especially on Flag Day," explained a tourist from Prince Albert, Saskatchewan. "I couldn't believe I was seeing him in real life, so I asked him for an autograph. That's when he reached for my throat instead of my pen."

The RCMP will now provide round-the-clock bodyguard protection for anyone on Parliament Hill when the prime minister is in or around the area.

# Nunavut secedes from NWT after prolonged civil war

———— APRIL 1, 1999 ————

IQALUIT — A long and bloody conflict came to a historic end today when the independent territory of Nunavut was declared.

The war broke out several years ago after an argument between Dene and Inuit elders over the total number of words for snow turned violent. The conflict split communities and pitted brother against brother, husky against husky.

The civil war made headlines around the world for the particularly ruthless tactics employed by both sides, including staring directly at one another without breaking eye contact, high-speed dogsled chases, ear pulling, and muktuk stealing. There were also reports of trained polar bear attacks on civilian communities; however, both factions have denied employing such a heinous act.

Military experts feel the entire conflict could have been resolved much sooner if forces hadn't been able to see each other coming from a long way off. They cite the Inuit's "frozen earth" policy of kicking in igloos and sealing up ice-fishing holes as being particularly effective in the long run.

At one point, peacekeeping forces from the Yukon were dispatched in an unsuccessful attempt at reconciliation.

With new territorial lines now drawn, both sides face the challenge of mending relationships and working together on the upcoming whale harvest. Nunavut premier Paul Okalik and Northwest Territories premier Jim Antoine joined together in a ceremonial blanket toss as a show of solidarity.

At press time, the federal government expressed surprise at news of the peace deal, having just learned about the conflict in the first place. A spokesperson for the new territory insists that it had been petitioning the government on this matter the entire time, just as they've been saying for years.

# Doomsday cult leader sick of Y2K bandwagoners

——— DECEMBER 20, 1999 ———

GRAVENHURST, ON — Claiming to have predicted the world's destruction back in 1976, Church of the Solar Gundestrup leader Dorth Manylights today expressed his frustration with those who've only recently joined his doomsday cult.

Thirty-five people have become followers of Manylights's teachings in the past three months, quadrupling the membership. This has ruffled the feathers of some lifelong members and caused confusion among the roles at his co-op vegetable farm.

"The many moons orbiting the planet Kulkchun have determined that the last day of our existence will be December 31, 1999, but I'm afraid not all of my new followers have always believed that," explained the Wise and Glorious Leader as he sat inside his bunker. "I was first to predict that humankind will destroy itself when clocks revert back to the year 1900, causing a rupture in time and space and obliterating everyone except for me and my followers. Using the power of a Mayan goddess given to me during my visit to Mexico many years ago, I can use the forces of the sun and moon to shield my followers from the falling bombs and the fracturing of the present as we know it.

"Except for [new member] Dave; that guy will follow anything that sounds cool."

Making matters worse, Manylights says he'll have to purchase another school bus for the compound and sacrifice many more goats to prepare everyone for the inevitable Armageddon.

"It's hard to hear our Wise and Glorious Leader speak with all these new people proclaiming that they'll do anything to receive his love and protection," said cult member Gloria Bloomfield, who's been with the Church for over a decade. "Many of these Y2Kers think they can show up, give up all their possessions to the Church, drink some virgin sheep blood, and boom, they're suddenly believing they'll live until the year 3287 when we're liberated by the people of Razakashan after being occupied by the Blootinumpners.

How naive do these newbies think we are?"

# THE OTTAWA
# BEAVERTON

*"North America's Trusted Source of News."*

Kim Jong-il's Imjingak railroad connects North and and South Korea —and hearts. Page 13

VOL. 34 NO. 134 ••••     MONDAY, SEPT. 18, 2000     152 PAGES     50 CENTS (47¢ + G.S.T.)

# STOCKWELL DAY
## arrives in Parliament on a Jet Ski

OTTAWA—Canadian Alliance MP Stockwell Day buzzed past parliamentary security on his Yamaha Sea-Doo so that he'd arrive in time for his inaugural Question Period as leader of the Official Opposition.

Day certainly made his presence known to MPs and the press gallery by circling the Clerk and Table officers twice, revving his engine, and tearing up the green carpet as he skidded through Parliament. The new leader smiled at Prime Minister Jean Chrétien and the Liberal front bench before performing a wheelie stunt to the amazement and applause of Alliance MPs.

Day then dismounted the recreational watercraft and docked it beside his reserved seat opposite Chrétien. Unzipping the front of his wetsuit halfway, he asked his first question about the government's poor accounting practices in Human Resources Development Canada.

"Mr. Speaker, I have been travelling on this Sea-Doo since I left Red Deer a week ago," he began, still wet from the 3000-kilometre journey. "And every Canadian I came across, be they water skiers or booze-cruise enthusiasts, told me they were not in favour of the 'billion-dollar boondoggle.' When will this government finally be accountable to taxpayers?"

The new leader hopes to appeal to the cool-dads demographic as well as those who believe it's a sin to shop on Sunday.

# STUFF *You Should* probably REMEMBER

## (2000–2017)

"Hello, this call is from Elections Canada informing you that the location of your polling station has changed to the bottom of Niagara Falls." —RoboCaller 3000, May 2, 2011

Canadians woke up at the dawn of the new millennium to find that they had not been strangled to death by their computers. Technology, terrorism, and terrible music defined this era. Gay and lesbian Canadians won the right to marry, Canadian soldiers risked their lives in Afghanistan, and most people passed through this time staring at a screen.

# KEY DATES

### October 15, 2003
al-Qaeda plot to smile in Canadian
passport photo foiled by Passport Canada

### February 7, 2006
Prime Minister Stephen Harper promises
accountability and transparency to
only journalist permitted to attend
his first press conference

### July 29, 2008
Arcade Fire finally beats Broken
Social Scene for title of most
pretentious Canadian band

### December 20, 2008
Ontario government forces everyone
to buy $3.3 billion worth of GM and
Chrysler cars that didn't sell so well

### February 2, 2010
Vancouver Olympic Committee
scrambles to find snow

### April 12, 2014
Veterans Affairs Minister Julian
Fantino grants mental health benefits
to veterans of the War of 1812

### September 2, 2015
Coconut falls on NDP Leader
Thomas Mulcair's head causing
him to believe he's a Liberal

# Gander residents to stranded 9/11 passengers: "You can't leave"

***6600 grounded travellers already integrated into town, cast in community play***

———— SEPTEMBER 13, 2001 ————

GANDER, NFLD — Kind and caring Gander residents have reminded passengers stranded by the closure of U.S. airspace that they can never leave now and must integrate into their small Newfoundland community.

"The plane people must stay," said Gander mayor Claude Elliott in a mysterious monotone. "We must be overwhelmingly generous so that they will feel obliged to remain. We will welcome them into our homes, cook them supper, and dress them in our clothes."

Early reports indicate that the strategy of being so damned nice has already started to work, with several intermarriages between residents and passengers.

Fred Swartz, a Philadelphia businessman who was travelling from London to New York when his aircraft was redirected, has wed the daughter of an older couple he was staying with. "Well, I had to accept when they made the proposal—even though I already have a wife and kids back home. These people are so lovely that it's really hard to say no."

# National identity restored after gold medal hockey game win

———— FEBRUARY 24, 2002 ————

SALT LAKE CITY, UT — The Canadian men's Olympic hockey team has won gold at Salt Lake City, reigniting Canadians' abstract sense of cohesive belonging.

"The very future of our vague, ill-defined traditions and culture was at stake," captain Mario Lemieux said after the game. "So we knew we had to put it away in the third."

After the medals ceremony and the singing of "O Canada," citizens can once again identify themselves as proud Canucks, don the Maple Leaf wherever they go, and no longer lament living in a country that hasn't won an Olympic hockey gold medal since 1952.

Canadians back home can feel fully assured of the nation's superiority, since compared to other countries its Olympic team is good at putting a vulcanized rubber disc into a 183-centimetre net with a wooden stick.

"This is more important than Confederation, Tim Hortons, and beer combined," said a teary-eyed Tony Humphrey of Uxbridge, Ontario. "We're a country that has faced separation, economic uncertainty, and a terrible loss in the 1998 Nagano Olympics. If we hadn't won the gold, I wouldn't know who I was or what sense of shared history I have with my fellow citizens."

Saskatoon police generously offer free twilight country tours to homeless Native men

How to prevent al-Qaeda from getting into your bedroom

War on terror: Canadian military to be fully equipped by 2019

Céline Dion on the loose: Singer escapes Las Vegas captivity

Chinese-manufactured Canadian flag flies proudly over Ottawa

Conrad Black granted titular title "Lord Black of C-Block" by U.S. Department of Corrections

# Man with close ties to shawarma deported to Syria

***RCMP suspects Maher Arar of planning massive Levantine meat preparation, others suspected***

—— SEPTEMBER 28, 2002 ——

OTTAWA — A dual Canadian-Syrian citizen with known connections to an organized shawarma restaurant has been deported back to Syria by U.S. authorities.

Maher Arar was detained by the U.S. Immigration and Naturalization Service in New York after it received a tip from the RCMP that Arar may have been attending a shawarma training camp in Tunis. It is unclear whether Arar was attempting to smuggle any flatbread into the country.

According to sources within

the security community, Arar was fingered by those already in custody who claimed that he often consumes the Middle Eastern dish, holds the belief that adding tahini sauce is a must, and is associated with radicals who subscribe to the same diet.

RCMP officers who raided Arar's home yesterday revealed that the shawarma sympathizer had been stockpiling container after container of hummus in preparation for a massive event that could have targeted friends and families at mealtime.

"We removed what we believe to be detailed instructions on how to make baklava and rice pudding, the same things that many terrorists eat," explained a Mountie spokesman.

Authorities are confident that Mr. Arar's deportation was necessary, as "he was already guilty of being an Arab."

---

# The SARSstock concert was totally worth the SARS I got

*By Duane Wilson*

—— JULY 31, 2003 ——

Dude, I have never in my life been to a more kickass concert than SARSstock. It was legendary, it was wicked, it made me not care about nearly dying from SARS.

There was an amazing list of people: Dan Aykroyd, the Rolling Stones, and so many more. They had even more amazing and talented musicians than there were talented doctors and nurses trying to figure out what I was suffering from when I arrived in the ER that night!

The place was packed like a lung filled to the brim with fluid from atypical pneumonia. This was Toronto's Woodstock, and everyone was congregating to spread the infectious lyrics of AC/DC and the Guess Who.

That drum solo by Neil Peart was so, so hot, like my 104°C body temperature as I lay in a negative-pressure ICU bed. He just kept going and going as if he were a machine that wouldn't stop, like the mechanical ventilator at North York General Hospital that kept me alive. Balls-to-the-walls awesome!

Keith Richards wailed on his

guitar during "Miss You," like my mom did while she sat just outside my isolated unit. Or at least that's what people told me. I was so out of it!

Of course, we all had to boo Justin Timberlake's performance. Everyone started throwing water bottles and muffins at him. Why did this guy even show up in the second half when he was so totally useless? That's like trying to treat a deadly virus with antibiotics when there's no actual cure. But it didn't ruin a thing for me.

I'm really looking forward to Toronto's Ebolastock!

# Chrétien's Letter to President Bush Declining "Coalition of the Willing" Invite

CANADA

PRIME MINISTER · PREMIER MINISTRE

Ottawa, Ontario
K1A 0A2

March 18, 2003

Dear George:

How are things? I hope your preparations for the war in Iraq are going well. We really do need to get rid of Saddam Hussein, as he's not a very nice fellow.

Speaking of which, I have to politely decline your considerate invitation to the invasion event. We're really busy that week. I don't mean to disappoint you or Tony, but my sister-in-law's brother's niece will be visiting and I can't miss an episode of *The Sopranos*. Oh, and many of our military units are already fighting in Afghanistan. Please let me know the next time you plan on invading and we'll try our best to make it. Say hi to Dick for me. Best of luck! The invasion will go well, I'm sure.

Your pal,

*Jean Chrétien*

President George Walker Bush
1600 Pennsylvania Ave NW,
Washington, DC
20500, USA

## Chrétien makes par after lucky bounce off Justice Gomery's head

-------- FEBRUARY 8, 2005 --------

OTTAWA — Former prime minister Jean Chrétien made a wild shot off Justice John Gomery's head while playing a round of golf at the inquiry into the sponsorship scandal.

The man who'd been prime minister during the operation of a corrupt government program that gave millions to Liberal-friendly ad firms had a difficult shot to make on the ninth hole.

Instead of using a soft chip into Gomery's glass of water, the PM—who denied any knowledge of illegal activities in what he called a "necessary program"—made a line drive with his three-wood directly into the justice's face, using a golf ball that Bill Clinton gave him.

"Fore!" shouted Chrétien, who took a massive swing that sent the ball directly between Gomery's eyes, knocking off his spectacles and then ricocheting off chairs, a television camera, and a table before plunking into the now dazed justice's water glass.

## Danes invade Canada over Hans Island dispute

-------- MAY 10, 2005 --------

TORONTO — Canada's dispute with Denmark over Hans Island, an unoccupied Arctic knoll barely larger than a square kilometre, has led to an all-out war between the two countries.

In a daring attack, Danish soldiers disguised as tourists stormed Parliament, the Supreme Court, and National Defence Headquarters. Reports indicate that Prime Minister Paul Martin narrowly avoided capture thanks to the heroics of a stalwart Mountie who pinned down 20 Danish barbarians with his bare hands to give the PM time to escape.

Canadian troops have prevented Danish forces from advancing to Montreal by placing red lights and Don't Walk signs along their route—exploiting the Danes' one well-known weakness: traffic-rule obedience.

In response to the Danes' flagrant violence, Canada has deployed thousands of parked cars to Copenhagen's bike lanes, causing widespread inconvenience.

Doing its part in the war effort, Tim Hortons restaurants throughout the country have renamed their Danishes "Patriot Pastries."

# Newfoundlanders defend controversial seasonal bludgeoning of Paul McCartney

JANUARY 12, 2006

ST. JOHN'S — Newfoundlanders are steadfastly supporting the annual clubbing of former Beatle and animal rights activist Sir Paul McCartney.

Premier Danny Williams noted that it's been a long-standing tradition; McCartney arrives every spring to lecture Newfoundlanders and the world about the cruelties of the seal hunt.

"This practice is highly regulated and even endorsed by Phil Collins," explained Williams on CNN's *Larry King Live*. "Our McCartney clubbing industry employs thousands, and it's a festivity that really brings the community together by reminding them of who they hate."

However, self-righteous celebrity rights organizations say that the long-held McCartney hunt is barbaric and impedes on a famous person's right to take up a cause they know little about.

"He's an adorable-looking Beatle, and there are only two Beatles remaining," said Allan Shepherd of Celebrities for Causes. "Why would anyone want to bludgeon a musician with such big, appealing eyes?"

Shepherd added that there are only 15,938 celebrities in the world willing to shamelessly support something their spouse is really passionate about.

"We need very important people like Paul around to remind us of what we should care about and also to expand name and brand recognition. For instance, Bono's brand is so strong that he's designated as a protected species whenever he visits starving children in Africa."

Meanwhile, on the sea ice, McCartney was starting to understand why John Lennon did all his protesting from a hotel room bed."

## Election 2006: Quotes

—

"Look, had I known about the sponsorship beforehand, I would have covered it up."
**PRIME MINISTER PAUL MARTIN**

"If you gaze into my cold, dead eyes, you will turn into stone."
**CONSERVATIVE LEADER STEPHEN HARPER**

"Union rules say that I can have a 15-minute break in the middle of this debate."
**NDP LEADER JACK LAYTON**

"Quebec sovereignty isn't dead; it's just resting its eyes."
**BLOC QUÉBÉCOIS LEADER GILLES DUCEPPE**

## BlackBerry Smartphone

*The BlackBerry, a smartphone produced by Waterloo-based Research in Motion (later renamed BlackBerry Limited), was very popular in the mid-2000s. The phone is still popular among historical re-enactors and may experience a resurgence with hipsters in the 2040s.*

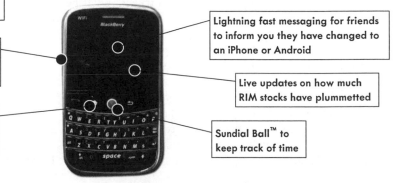

Not Shown: 10 km-long charge cord so your phone can stay on while you travel for 10 km

Total Weight: 25 lbs. Good substitute as an anchor for small watercraft

Press this button to make Research in Motion CEO Jim Balsille appear

Lightning fast messaging for friends to inform you they have changed to an iPhone or Android

Live updates on how much RIM stocks have plummeted

Sundial Ball™ to keep track of time

## Peter MacKay sends makeup, high heels to oppressed women in Afghanistan

———— OCTOBER 6, 2008 ————

KANDAHAR — Defence Minister Peter MacKay has ordered that $30 million worth of makeup, high heels, fashion magazines, and other "ladies" products be deployed to Afghanistan, saying that women haven't had access to such items under the Taliban regime.

"As someone who knows women, I take this issue very personally," announced the defence minister. "Canadian ladies take for granted many womanly luxuries, such as having a night out with the girls or watching *The Bachelor*. Afghan women have lived under such a horrific regime that it's never reminded them

A Canadian C-17 loaded with stilettos, make-up, and other female liberation supplies, arrives in Kabul

how beautiful they really are."

He went on to point out that no one has taught Afghan women how to be liberated, but that he believes this generous donation from the Department of National Defence should do the trick.

"Blush, not burqas," declared a stoic MacKay. "Women haven't been able to wear mascara or pencil skirts under the Taliban. Now they can feel confident

that a man will take the time to compliment them on how good they look. This female liberation is exactly what our troops are fighting for."

The Canadian International Development Agency said that it will offer Afghan women free CDs of Shania Twain's third studio album *Come On Over*, featuring the 1997 hit "Man! I Feel Like a Woman!"

# Harper government offers apology to victims of long-form census

———— JUNE 18, 2010 ————

OTTAWA — Prime Minister Stephen Harper has issued an official apology to victims of the long-form census, offering financial compensation to the millions of Canadians who had to deal with it every five years.

"There were 6.4 million households traumatized by the questions this census asked," a solemn Harper announced. "Many had to fill out several additional responses while family members watched on helplessly or were forced to participate. Year after year, we asked 20% of Canadians to do

what no other Canadian had to do: answer extra questions. On behalf of the Canadian government, I am truly sorry."

The federal government has already taken measures to protect citizens from the horrors of a long-form census by making it a voluntary survey. It acknowledged, however, that this would not erase the pain previously suffered.

"I still get nightmares about my experience," said Kurt Flanigan of Regina. "I remember that day in May 2006 like it was yesterday. When I opened the census in the mail, it was a lot heavier than usual. I knew I had

no way of getting out of it. The law obliged me to fill things in."

A hush came over the crowd in the House of Commons foyer as the 45-year-old construction worker told his heart-wrenching story.

"It forced me to . . . to give information . . . about . . . my form of . . . transportation to work," sobbed Flanigan. "It had no right to ask something like that! I feel so violated and dirty!"

Industry Minister Tony Clement consoled Flanigan with a hug, saying repeatedly, "It's not your fault . . . It's not your fault."

# Margaret Atwood goes part-time at Starbucks to pursue writing passion

———— MARCH 2, 2012 ————

TORONTO — Renowned Canadian author and full-time barista Margaret Atwood is taking some time away from her busy work schedule at Starbucks to focus on her writing career.

The 2000 Booker Prize winner and author of dozens of novels, short stories, and poetry collections says she just had to dive in and pursue her passion if she was ever going to make it.

"But I'll still be working 25 hours a week so that I can afford rent," said Atwood as she poured an espresso shot into a grande low-fat caramel macchiato.

Finding time off work has been difficult for one of Canada's most prolific writers. Last week, Atwood missed receiving an honorary degree from McGill when she had to cover a colleague's shift.

"Carolyn [Atwood's assistant manager] would allow me to do part-time only if I took all morning shifts and was available on call," said the author of *Alias Grace*, *The Year of the Flood*, and *The Handmaid's Tale*.

In related news, Lawrence Hill was recently fired from his call-centre position after signing books during his five-minute coffee break.

# DAVID SUZUKI'S SEVEN SIMPLE THINGS YOU CAN DO TO SAVE THE ENVIRONMENT

JUNE 13, 2012

## 1. Turn off the light when you leave the room.
It's such an easy thing to do. Whenever you begin to leave a room, take a moment and ask yourself: Will I be re-entering this room in less than half a second? If not, switch it off! Every light left burning is more hydro used, more fish habitats ruined, and more First Nations communities irreversibly displaced. Want to go the extra mile? Consider investing in some earwax-candle supplies. Even better, work, read, and play only when there's enough natural light.

## 2. Prevent friends, family, colleagues, neighbours, and anyone else from driving.
I've heard people complain about this: "How can I stop others from causing irreparable damage to the air we breathe?" It's simple: by force. Cut your neighbour's brakes, drain Sally Sue's oil from her car, slash your mother's tires, and lie down in the middle of the road at the end of your street. Sure, you might say, but won't they just get around these tactics and get back on the road? Not if you're vigilant. Keep at it!

## 3. Negotiate an international carbon tax agreement.
Work with provincial, federal, and international agents to finally hammer out a carbon tax agreement to which all are held accountable. Develop a consensus on how to implement it, ensuring that all checks and balances are in place to monitor its execution.

## 4. Force major banks to divest from resource-extraction and other unethical funds.
Implement a policy requiring that public and private financial services divest from fossil fuel interests. Simply rally all corporations, institutions, and individuals across the globe to break the hold fossil fuels have on our governments and economies. Complete divestment is the goal. You can do it!

## 5. Overthrow the capitalist system, since it perpetuates mass consumption in order to maximize profits for the few at the expense of environmental and human health.
Today's ecological crisis is in many ways tied to this relentless pursuit of profits. The environment as a whole—a beautiful, highly complex balancing of nutrients, carbons, and all other elements in a self-renewing cycle—was derailed by the 19th-century onset of the Industrial Revolution, which ramped up human production and consumption with the invention of fossil fuel–capturing energy sources. Today, the effects of capitalism on the environment are compounded by globalization and hyper-consumer tendencies. Get to the root of ecological destruction by returning humanity to its roots—agrarian roots, that is.

## 6. Kill everyone you know.
Humans are the most destructive animals on the planet. Culling a few billion would really help out other species. Then we might have a chance.

## 7. Take sailor showers.
Get wet for a few seconds and then turn your shower off. Soap up and quickly rinse afterward. By having two-minute showers, you can reduce the overall impact of water consumption.

## Government-Issued Ballgag

*Standard issue for all government scientists and federal public servants, this ballgag was to be worn 24 hours a day in order to prevent any leaks or contradictions on policy. A blindfold was also issued to anyone working on climate change.*

## Toronto Mayor Rob Ford's Crack Pipe

## Dozens survive hour-long Wi-Fi outage

———— APRIL 14, 2014 ————

VANCOUVER — A harrowing ordeal unfolded at a downtown Vancouver coffee shop yesterday when its Wi-Fi was abruptly disconnected, leaving 25 customers and 4 employees cut off from the internet.

Witnesses describe the scene as a heroic tale of survival that lasted for nearly 60 full minutes.

"I don't have much data left on my phone," said a woman in her 20s who was visibly hyperventilating. "What do I do? I just bought my frappuccino and sat down in the only comfortable chair available. Where's the free Wi-Fi?!"

After the first three minutes of the outage, alarm began to set in. Some even texted their final farewells to friends and family as they huddled in their chairs and tried to avoid eye contact with fellow customers. Others tried standing on crates to see whether another Wi-Fi connection was in range, but they were locked out.

"If I don't make it out of here alive, can someone tell my girlfriend that I liked her cat video on Facebook?" asked a panicking young man who began to sob. "Why couldn't I have gone to that other Starbucks across the street?"

When the internet was finally restored, survivors were still shaken. Most planned on rehabilitating themselves by staring at a screen for the next 10 minutes.

# Government removes "Trans" from Trans-Canada Highway, citing family values

———— DECEMBER 3, 2014 ————

OTTAWA, ON — Canada's transcontinental highway will get a name change after several Conservative MPs and senators expressed discomfort with the current name.

The Conservative caucus accused the name of being part of the longstanding LGBTQ agenda, which is being forced down the throats of Canadian families every time they drive.

"There are tens of thousands of signs that say 'Trans' on them," explained Conservative Senator Don Plett. "This is simply liberal propaganda corrupting everyone's mind. We need a new name that reflects real Canadian values that are as straight as a drive through Saskatchewan."

Other Conservatives were also worried about how the 8030 km stretch of highway, with its many interchanges, was damaging the minds of the nation's youth.

"An eastbound driver can't wake up one day and decide that they're suddenly a westbound driver," said Conservative MP Rob Anders. "Children need to be protected from drivers who think it's okay to go both ways."

In addition to the name change, the government announced the construction of a new roadside washroom where Rob Anders will personally check every patron's genitals to verify they're in the right washroom.

# Some guy who is not Stephen Harper wins election

———— OCTOBER 19, 2015 ————

OTTAWA — A guy whose father used to be prime minister has defeated Stephen Harper and will form the next government.

The leader of a party that is not Conservative won a majority government, including every seat in Atlantic Canada, mostly because of his campaign promise to not be Stephen Harper.

"Sunny ways, my friends, sunny ways," said the 43-year-old man who bears no resemblance to the iron-fisted 28th prime minister. "A Canadian is a Canadian is a Canadian."

Most of those on the left and in the centre had agreed to vote strategically for the man with the stylish hair instead of the other guy with the beard.

"I feel relieved that Harper will no longer use the politics of division to run our country," one progressive remarked. "And it turns out that the person I voted for is also a feminist and acknowledges that climate change is a problem. Well, that's a plus, I guess."

# Justin Trudeau vows to photo-bomb every Canadian by 2019

———— AUGUST 4, 2016 ————

OTTAWA — Prime Minister Justin Trudeau has vowed to accidentally place himself in the selfies, portraits, and wedding photographs of all 36 million Canadians by 2019.

"I have listened to Canadians and they want to see their prime minister represented in their beach vacation or high school prom," announced Trudeau. "I may not be able to reform the electoral system, or balance the budget by 2019, but I am well on my way to butting into the background of images while performing some spontaneous recreational activity."

The prime minister, known for appointing the first gender balanced cabinet in Canadian history, said that he has a variety of poses and outfits ready for the serendipitous moments. Seven million Canadians have already had their images photobombed by Trudeau at 293 family BBQs, two funerals, and a colonoscopy.

"And it will only be coincidence that my photographer will be nearby just in case Canadians miss that ideal shot of me," added Trudeau.

---

**ASK A HOCKEY EXPERT**

Q. What is a "Sidney Crosby Hat Trick"?

A. A goal, an assist, and a concussion.

## Green party elects its first hyper-intelligent compost heap as leader

**VICTORIA** — In what's being called a milestone, the Greens have elected an intelligent organic waste heap as leader.

The candidate, who dwells in a Vancouver backyard, beat out its competitors on the second ballot after wooing enough David Suzuki Jr. supporters away from the endangered marmot camp. In the end, the steaming pile of grass, eggshells, and fruit and vegetable peels won by a sizable 63% margin.

The heap campaigned on promises to give back to the soil, develop a robust waste-management policy, and halt freshwater pipeline developments to California.

The leadership bid was not without controversy. The compost heap had a history of emitting methane gas, attracting fruit fly infestations, and demonstrating lukewarm support for electoral reform.

Nevertheless, the newly minted leader had an upbeat attitude about the Greens' prospects for winning a government.

According to sources within the party, the leader's first task will be to slowly decompose old party policy for a richer protozoa count.

# ADDENDUM

(2017–2167)

"This will be the last federal election conducted under the first-past-the-post voting system." —Prime Minister Hadrien Trudeau, October 12, 2062

We here at *The Beaverton* have developed a highly sophisticated machine that can foretell what will happen in Canada over the next 150 years. And by "sophisticated machine" we mean that we've observed the innards of a dead beaver and, in the haruspicy tradition, have made predictions based on what its liver looks like. Here are some stories you might read when the updated version of this book is released in 2167.

# KEY DATES

**April 22, 2032**
38.3% of Quebec separates from
Canada after first proportional
representation referendum

**May 4, 2034**
Average tsunami-devastated home
in Vancouver costs $3 million

**July 28, 2044**
Alberta government worried first
trans-continental water pipeline to U.S.
may rupture, contaminate oil sands

**March 12, 2050**
First Nations majority in Saskatchewan:
White people begin transition to
suburban reserve system

**February 21, 2071**
Canada's first AI politician embroiled in
scandal after using taxpayer's batteries,
power supply for personal use

**October 16, 2092**
Giant pandas, now an invasive
species, have eaten over half
of Canada's boreal forest

# Canada wins three bronze, one silver in first random-participant Olympics

DAMASCUS — As the 43rd Olympiad comes to a close in the first-ever competition based on selecting random citizens to represent their respective countries, Canada has racked up a total of four medals.

"It was a good workout, one I haven't had in a while," said bronze medallist and administrative assistant Cheryl Burnside from Canmore, Alberta, who ran the 400 metre in under five minutes. "I really broke a sweat, and didn't think I was going to make it. Then I collapsed passing the finish line, but when I finally regained consciousness I was told I'd come in third."

The IOC mandated random athlete selection in order to avoid earlier controversies involving genetic engineering, illegal bionics, neuropriming, and every Russian athlete suspiciously medalling in the 2052 Toronto Olympics. Professional and amateur athletes alike are barred from competition to prevent any further cheating. Once selected, all citizens are obliged to participate regardless of their weight or fitness level.

Marc-André Filliol of Sherbrooke, Quebec, secured Canada a silver medal in the 10-metre platform dive with an impressive half-spin belly flop in his last plunge, narrowly missing gold in the final points.

"I was happy to do it for my country," said the 42-year-old in a neck brace.

Total Olympics viewership hit a record 3 billion, with many from around the world entertained by the spectacle of ordinary people struggling to engage in athletic competition. Adding to the enjoyment was the chance to evaluate each country's fitness standards rather than having wealth or performance-enhancing drugs determine medal count.

Overall, Bangladesh came out as the country with the most medals at 42, followed by Mozambique at 39 and Mongolia at 38.

This was the first year in which the U.S. team failed to medal in any sport, with most American athletes struggling to breathe during their competitions or failing to complete their events.

---

ADDENDUM | 189

---

# Another bumper harvest for Nunavut wheat, mangoes

IQALUIT — Thanks to soaring temperatures and advanced genetic engineering, Nunavut Wheat Corporation has posted another record harvest in wheat and exotic fruit.

Wheat threshers and foreign labourers from Australia were seen tending the fields outside Canada's Arctic capital, whose population is nearing 1 million.

"Nunavut's mild winters, hot summers, and lack of drought puts us on top of deserts like California or Saskatchewan," explained Nunavut premier Dale Okalik. "This has really been a boon, given that there are no longer any narwhals, Arctic char, polar bears, or . . . well, any native species that aren't already extinct. But these bananas are delicious."

Since the territory hasn't seen snow in approximately 10 years owing to climate change, Nunavut's sandy beaches are now a popular destination for tourists from devastated places like New York and Vancouver.

"It's really nice not having to walk around in water all day, and the sun stays up all night during the summer," said Farshid Singh, a visitor from the floodplains of Victoria. "I never realized how humid the North was until I got up here."

# Tories oppose death-ray gun registry

OTTAWA — The Judeo-Christian Conservative party has made it clear to the governing Green Democrats that they plan to oppose any form of registry for those who possess death-ray guns.

The federal government has been examining a proposal to ensure that every weaponized beam that can fry millions to death in an instant be registered. The move comes after half of New Brunswick was obliterated by an unknown villain.

"Any registration would go after law-abiding meteor hunters and mad-science enthusiasts," explained Tory Jayston Alliwix Woncatha, MP for Calgary Centre-West-Centre. "We'd be punishing people who use their directed-energy weapons responsibly. Everyone has the right to own and operate one of these safe devices."

During the debate, the Tories noted that death-ray gun owners already have to acquire a licence, pass their psychiatrist's background sanity check, and take a half-day death-ray-gun course.

However, the government said that its proposed registry will help law enforcement flee in time before they're incinerated by a 5000°C laser.

"This will really help protect police officers by alerting them of their impending doom," said Safe Communities Minister Alan Faust Arsenault. "Plus, their screams for mercy will let others know."

## Jasper's mountains painted blue, white in memory of real glacier

JASPER NATIONAL PARK, AB — Parks Canada announced that, using simulated glacier colours, it has painted over the Columbia Icefield Area and the Athabasca Glacier in an effort to remind sightseers that ice once existed in the park.

The task required over 200 million litres of white and blue paint, but thanks to aerial spraying by computerized drones and water bombers, the job was completed within a few days.

"We're quite happy with how the project turned out," said Lysander Brookes, a landscape artist who was responsible for designing the massive memorial. "The optical illusion is meant to illustrate that the temperature was once cold enough to sustain a consistent amount of ice. We based this illusion on a photo

from 1998, which accurately captured what people saw at that time."

Many of those visiting the area were happy that the glaciers were back and that they wouldn't be melting any time soon.

"I remember when my parents brought me here in their RV in the summer of 2017," said 90-year-old Madison Wilson, wiping tears from her eyes. "There used to be something called 'snowcaps,' which made the mountains white. The rivers used to be an emerald blue filled with freshwater rather than grey rocks and fish bones."

But, as with most public art, there were some critics.

"It's really inconsistent with

the rest of the park," said Olaf Meusner, who'd never seen an interpretation of a glacier in his life. "It really goes against the arid dead-land mystique of Jasper, which is what it's known for."

The installation is planned as a permanent exhibit, but much like the Golden Gate Bridge, which sadly collapsed in 2051, the mountains will require an annual paint touch-up.

# Last journalist replaced with Advertorial Bot 5000 (Brought to You by Automaton Communication Technologies)

JULY 2, 2167

TORONTO — The only remaining newspaper in Canada has finally let go of its last human reporter and adopted a more efficient, technologically proven system by purchasing an Advertorial Bot 5000.

The *Beaverton National Star Post and Mail,* Canada's sole media conglomerate, has completely automated all its written material with Automaton Communication Technologies.

"This was a step in the right direction for our organization," explained *Nat-Star-Post* publisher Alix Singh. "People need more information on what to buy or what corporation is doing good work in their community."

By using a complex analysis of social media, an Advertorial Bot 5000 can produce 10 stories per second that Canadians think are real news. It can be programmed to meet any deadline, features dramatic, eye-catching headlines, and includes over 2000 entertaining listicle formats. Unlike the Automated Journalists brand, the Advertorial Bot 5000 follows leads in product placements and the next "It" offerings.

"I no longer have to deal with messy union negotiations or incompetent interns," Singh said. "With the Advertorial Bot 5000, I don't need to hire reporters or scribes to promote the hottest brands or the good work that an oil company is doing in Arctic communities."

## Today's Pipeline Ruptures

Trans-Mountain: B.C. Interior

Line 3: South Saskatchewan River

Never-Bust Pipeline: Algonquin Park

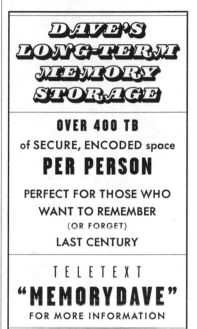
ADDENDUM | 191

—30—

# CONCLUSION AND APOLOGIES

Thank you for reading *The Beaverton Presents: Glorious and/or Free*, or at least receiving it as a gift and placing it in your bookshelf, convincing yourself that you may one day feel the need to read War of 1812 jokes. By now, you have a firm grasp on all of the important events and people who shaped this wonderful country. We encourage you to apply what you have learned so we don't repeat the same mistakes our ancestors made, or the mistakes we are making right now.

As a proud Canadian tradition, we would like to apologize to anyone and everyone who was offended by our gross perversion of Canada's history. In particular, we would like to say sorry to military historians, the Melville Heritage Museum, the City of Melville, the people of Melville, all Twitter accounts who were/will be offended, the Canadian Historical Association, Brock University, Canadian Studies students, the Royal Ontario Museum (in our defence, many of those irreplaceable artifacts had been disintegrating before we broke them), the trees used to print this book, Library and Archives Canada, Mr. Singh's grade 9 history class, the people who think this apology bit has gone on too long, and the man in a silver 2009 Hyundai Santa Fe with Ontario plates who honked at us for waiting a half second too long while the traffic light was turning green.

With this book now complete, we encourage you to go out there and make some Canadian history of your own so we have something to write about in our next book.[1]

The Editors

---

1 But please, try not to do anything terrible like starting wars, desecrating the environment, or trying to clone Kevin O'Leary.

# ACKNOWLEDGMENTS

This book would not have been possible without the kind assistance and permission of many archives and collections. Thank you to Library and Archives Canada, Denise Grant Photography, Whitehorse Public Library, Julie Grahame/The Estate of Yousef Karsh, Queen's University Archives, Provincial Archives of Saskatchewan, Halifax Municipal Archives, City of Vancouver Archives, and the City of Toronto Archives for helping us locate some remarkable historical books, images, and illustrations.

Thank you also to Mark Swartz at Queen's University Library for advising us on copyright law, to Alex's uncle, David Huntley, for allowing him to crash at his place in Toronto, and to all of the Beaverton writers who continue to satirize our nation daily.

Thank you to our fantastic book agent, Sam Hiyate, and the team at Penguin Random House—in particular, Five Seventeen, who designed the book, helped research images, and lent Photoshop expertise.

And a special thank you to the team at Bell Media for their support of the Beaverton.

# CREDITS CONTINUED

**ALEX HUNTLEY** is an editor and senior writer with *The Beaverton*. Born and raised in Niagara, he earned a BA with Honours in politics and history and a Master's in Public Administration from Queen's University, and has an expired basic first aid certificate from the distinguished school of St. John's Ambulance. Since joining *The Beaverton* in 2012, this government policy analyst turned comedy writer has expanded the publication's presence in Canada by living in Montreal, Whitehorse, and exotic Winnipeg while recruiting local writers. Having a love affair with Canadian history since childhood, he created *The Beaverton*'s Moments in Canadian History in 2013. Writing a book satirizing the nation's story is a dream come true. He lives with his wife in Kingston.

**LUKE GORDON FIELD** is editor-in-chief of the Beaverton website and co-executive producer of the critically acclaimed Beaverton television series. After attending Upper Canada College, Luke studied Canadian History at Queen's University, graduating with distinction. He then completed his JD at Osgoode Hall Law School and took the next logical step: becoming a stand-up comedian and comedy writer. As a stand-up he has had the pleasure of touring all over Canada and very specific parts of America. His greatest passion remains *The Beaverton*, which he has run since 2012, helping it become the culturally dominant media empire it is today. He knows an absurd amount of trivia about William Lyon McKenzie King, and would be happy to tell you some if you'll listen.